NO PLOT?
NO PROBLEM!

NO PLOT?

NO PROBLEM!

A LOW-STRESS, HIGH-VELOCITY GUIDE TO
WRITING A NOVEL IN 30 DAYS

CHRIS BATY
FOUNDER OF
NATIONAL NOVEL WRITING MONTH

CHRONICLE BOOKS
SAN FRANCISCO

Library of Congress Cataloging-in-Publication Data available.

ISBN 978-1-4521-2477-3

Manufactured in Canada.

Design and illustrations by Tatiana Pavlova.

10 9 8 7 6 5 4 3 2 1

Chronicle Books LLC
680 Second Street
San Francisco, California 94107

www.chroniclebooks.com

FOR MY PARENTS,
who knew it was possible
all along.

CONTENTS

SECTION TWO

WRITE HERE! WRITE NOW! A FRANTIC, FANTASTIC WEEK-BY-WEEK OVERVIEW TO BASHING OUT YOUR BOOK

PREFACE TO THE REVISED, UPDATED, AND EXPANDED EDITION

So much has changed since *No Plot? No Problem!* first rolled off the presses in 2004. Ebooks and print-on-demand technologies have opened publishing to thousands of new voices. Social media has dramatically expanded the writer's tool kit, allowing anyone with a great idea to get distracted by cat videos and high school friends' vacation photos at any hour of the day.

And National Novel Writing Month—the literary marathon I was shoestringing out of my living room ten years ago—has grown into a year-round nonprofit with a staff, an office, and 450,000 participants annually. The flagship autumn event has been joined by a virtual novel-writing camp in summer (www.campnanowrimo.org) and a classroom-based Young Writers Program that is now taught in over 1,000 schools.

It's been a wonderful, crazy decade. In that time, I've stumbled upon a host of new strategies to help you fit a book into the middle of your busy life. In this Revised, Updated, and Expanded Edition of *No Plot? No Problem!*, you'll find fresh advice on everything from taming digital distractions to mixing authorhood with parenthood to revising your novel without losing your mind. I've added weekly recaps and nearly a hundred fantastic new tips from NaNoWriMo winners. I've also commissioned several creativity-boosting, stress-reducing pep talks from some of the authors who have taken their books from the NaNoWriMo finish line to the *New York Times* bestseller list.

This Revised, Updated, and Expanded Edition also gives me the chance to correct a few, uh, misstatements that appeared in the original version of *No Plot? No Problem!* It was wrong of me, for example, to suggest that writers who use the second-person point-of-view will be driven from their homes by pitchfork-wielding mobs. The biggest error in the 2004 edition, though, was my naïve claim that everyone has a novel in them. With an additional decade of NaNoWriMo under my belt, I can safely say that everyone does not have a novel in them.

Everyone has *dozens* of novels in them. And getting one of those stories written is even more fun and life-changing than I had originally realized. Even after so many years, I still look forward to NaNoWriMo with an embarrassing amount of excitement. Whether you're about to write your first or your fifteenth novel, I hope this Revised, Updated, and Expanded Edition of *No Plot? No Problem!* serves as a trusty companion for an unforgettable month of literary abandon.

INTRODUCTION

The era, in retrospect, was very kind to dumb ideas.

The year was 1999, and I was working as a writer in the San Francisco Bay Area, drinking way too much coffee and watching the dot-com boom rewrite the rules of life around me.

Back then, it seemed entirely possible that my friends and I would spend three years in the workforce—throwing Nerf balls at each other and staging office-chair races—and then cash in our hard-earned stock options, buy a small island somewhere, and helicopter off into blissful retirement.

It was a delicious, surreal moment, and in the middle of it all I decided that what I really needed to do was write a novel in a month. Not because I had a great idea for a book. On the contrary, I had no ideas for a book.

All of this made perfect sense in 1999.

In a more grounded age, my novel-in-a-month concept would have been reality-checked right out of existence. Instead, the very first National Novel Writing Month set sail two weeks later, with almost everyone I knew in the Bay Area on board.

That the twenty-one of us who signed up for the escapade were undertalented goofballs who had no business flailing around at the serious endeavor of novel writing was pretty clear. We hadn't taken any creative writing courses in college, or read any how-to books on story or craft. And our combined post-elementary-school fiction output would have fit comfortably on a Post-it note.

My only explanation for our cheeky ambition is this: Being surrounded by pet-supply websites worth more than Apple had a way of getting your sense of what was possible all out of whack. The old millennium was dying; a better one was on its way. We were in our mid-twenties, and we had no idea what we were doing. But we knew we loved books. And so we set out to write them.

Bookish Hooligans →

That love of books, I think, was the saving grace of the whole enterprise. However unseriously we had agreed to take the writing process, we had an absolute reverence for novels themselves, the papery bricks of goodness that, once pried apart, unleashed the most amazing visions in their owners. In books, we'd found magical portals and steadfast companions, witnessed acts of true love and gaped at absolute evil. Books, as much as our friends and parents, had been our early educators, allowing us our first glimpses into life beyond the gates of childhood.

If we loved books, we were equally awestruck by their creators. Novelists were clearly a different branch of Homo sapiens; an enlightened subspecies endowed with an overdeveloped understanding of the human condition and the supernatural ability to spell words properly.

Novelists, we knew, had it made. They got fawned over in bookstores, and were forever being pestered for insights on their genius. They had license to dress horribly, wear decades-out-of-date hairstyles, and had their shortcomings interpreted as charming quirks and idiosyncrasies rather than social dysfunctions.

Best of all, novel writing was, for them, a lifetime sport—one of the few branches of the entertainment industry where you are allowed to have a career long after you've stopped looking good in hot pants.

In short, we adored novels and glorified writers, and thought that if, after a month's labors, we could claim even the thinnest of alliances with that world, something mysterious and transformational would happen to us. The possibility of starting the month with nada and ending it with a book we'd written—no matter how bad that book might be—was irresistible. And, though we never admitted it to one another, there was also the hope that maybe, just maybe, we'd yank an undeniable work of genius from the depths of our imagination. A masterpiece-in-the-rough that would forever change the literary landscape. The Accidental American Novel. Just think of the acclaim! The feelings of satisfaction! The vastly increased dating opportunities!

The power this last point held over us, sadly, is not to be underestimated. As a music nerd, I *knew* it could happen. The annals of rock 'n' roll are filled with self-taught musicians who recorded albums first and learned how to play their instruments much later. The Sex Pistols, the Ramones, Beat Happening—they were all inspirational examples of unpolished, untrained people who went from nobodies to kings and queens of their oeuvre through sheer exuberance.

If fantasies of screaming, headbanging fans forming mosh pits at our book signings were flitting through our minds in 1999, though, we weren't admitting it to anyone. Officially, this whole whirlwind novel-writing thing was to be an exercise in slapdash mediocrity. The more you wrote and the less you pretended to care, the better your standing in the field.

So at the dawn of the first National Novel Writing Month we laughed and toasted one another's complete lack of preparation and dismal chances of success with gusto. Much like novice sailors making good on a drunken dare, we were sailing out to sea on an already-sinking ship.

And that, on July 1, 1999, was how National Novel Writing Month began: twenty-one of us waving merrily to well-wishers gathered on shore, blowing kisses at our friends and family as we secretly cast nervous glances around the deck for life rafts.

We had no idea at the time how soon we'd end up needing them.

A Month at Sea →

Writer and championship figure skater Ralph Waldo Emerson once wrote, "In skating over thin ice, our safety is in our speed." As we hurled ourselves toward our likely literary demise, we were nothing if not quick about it.

The opening week of NaNoWriMo (as we were all soon calling it) was an overcaffeinated typing frenzy. For the sake of clarity, we had all agreed to define a novel as 50,000 words of fiction. With that lofty goal in sight, quantity quickly took precedence over quality, and we met in coffee shops after work each night to add another couple thousand words to our literary creations.

As we wrote, we gave ourselves word quotas and created elaborate challenges and races. Anyone who hadn't reached their writing goal wasn't allowed to get drink refills or go to the bathroom until they hit the mark. It was ridiculous, screaming fun, and the levity of those early sessions infused what would have normally been a terrifying endeavor—writing a book in an absurdly short amount of time—into a raucous field trip to Novel-land.

The rambunctious mood of those first few days was further buoyed by the fact that the writing campaign started off well for all of us. In short order, we had settings, main characters, and a few chapters under our belts. The hardest part was over, it seemed, and we settled into our novels confident that our muses would guide us through whatever unfamiliar terrain lay ahead.

Our muses, it turned out, had other plans.

Becalmed

By the seven-day mark, the initial excitement had worn off, and it revealed a sad and ugly truth: Our novels were bad. Maybe even horrible. As Week One slipped away, the intoxicating speed of the escapade ground to a halt, and we began poking at our novels with the dismay of a third-grader whose slice of cake has been swapped for a plate of vegetables.

When we broached the subject of our flagging enthusiasm during one of our writing sessions, it became clear that most of us were having the same problem: Starting had been easy. Continuing was hard. Perhaps flinging a random assortment of characters at a Word document, we admitted, was not the soundest approach to book building. And maybe trying to cram something as large as novel writing into an already busy schedule doomed both life and literature.

Our lives certainly had taken on the feel of cursed things: Giving over every free moment to our novels meant no sleeping in on weekends, no TV, and no meals with friends. Instead, we spent our downtime prodding at lifeless characters and wondering how long a human body could subsist on a diet of ramen and Coke before liver function ceased entirely.

By the middle of Week Two, we were ready to mutiny. Half of the participants dropped out. Unfortunately, some of us had bragged so widely about our heroic novel-writing quest that we were too ashamed to quit before the month ended. So we slogged on, continuing to meet for less-than-joyous writing sessions. We were no longer in it to win it; our plan at that point was just to run out the clock.

Week Two came and went. And then some strange things started happening.

The aimless, anemic characters we'd invented in the first fourteen days began to perk up and *do* things. Quirky, unexpected, readable things. They sold their SUVs and started commuting to work in golf carts. They joined polka bands and got kidnapped by woodland creatures and found themselves organizing jewel-heist capers with their next-door neighbors from the nursing home.

It was as if our protagonists, tired of waiting for competent stage direction from us, simply took control of the show. Thankfully, they turned out to be far better storytellers than we ever were.

The listlessness of Week Two lifted, and the flat lines of our novels began to resemble the trajectories of honest-to-God story arcs. We were still tired, sure. But our books had gone from being albatrosses around our necks to welcoming ports in the storm of everyday life. Rather than dreading the nightly drudgery of writing, we began fantasizing about what directions the story would take. We called our answering machines to dictate plot breakthroughs we'd hatched on our morning commutes, and scribbled out ever-lengthening backstories on napkins, receipts, coworkers—

anything we could get our hands on to capture some of the ideas that were pouring out of our brains.

To be fair, the novels emerging on our hard drives were far from the works of genius we'd secretly hoped for. They were stiff and awkward creatures, riddled with plot holes. But they were beautiful in their own way. And absolutely breathtaking in their potential.

If You Build It, Kevin Costner Will Come

Needless to say, at this point we were freaked out of our minds. It felt like we'd stumbled through a portal into a giddy netherworld, a Narnia for grown-ups where hours passed like seconds and the most outrageous and wonderful things you could imagine became real.

It was one of the best, most fulfilling experiences of my life, and, sadly, the only thing I can compare it to is the movie *Field of Dreams*—where Kevin Costner, playing an Iowa farmer, begins hearing voices that tell him: *"If you build it, they will come."*

At the advice of the creepy voices, Kevin distances himself from his nay-saying wife and does what any self-respecting man would do: He wrecks his cornfield and builds a baseball diamond next to his farmhouse. He's clearly berserk. Possessed. Crazy as a loon.

Those of us heading toward the fourth week of NaNoWriMo could relate.

In the movie, Costner's labors are rewarded with the appearance of ghostly baseball greats from bygone eras, who play exhibition games and inspire epiphanies in James Earl Jones. For us, the rewards were similarly bountiful. After two weeks of tilling the meager soil of our imaginations, the stories we'd been tending bloomed riotously. In Week Three, we harvested bumper crops of plot twists and fascinating characters, all of them eager to have their star turns on the sets we'd created.

Though undeniably lousy baseball players, they were good at other things. My characters, for example, were good at sleeping with people they weren't supposed to. Another person's characters were good at taking road trips. And someone else's were good at inventing fonts that, when viewed, made people's brains explode.

To each their own. Whatever varied directions our stories were moving in, they were definitely *moving*. And they were dragging us, happy and wide-eyed, in their wake.

On Day 29, the first participant crossed the 50,000-word finish line. Another followed. Then another. July came to a close, and as exhilarating as it had been to spend thirty-one days exploring the outer reaches of our imaginations, we were all ready to return to real life. So we wrapped up our stories, put our characters to bed, and turned out the lights one by one in the worlds we'd created.

Of the twenty-one people who participated, only six of us made it across the 50,000-word finish line that first year, with the rest falling short by anywhere from 500 to 49,000 words. Everyone who participated in the escapade, though, came away from the experience changed by it.

Some participants, to be honest, realized that they never wanted to write another book again. Others were ready to apply the next day to MFA programs in creative writing. For me, the revelation I couldn't shake was this: The biggest thing separating people from their artistic ambitions is not a lack of talent. It's the lack of a deadline. Give someone an enormous task, a supportive community, and a friendly-yet-firm due date, and miracles will happen every time.

Thanks to the go-go-go structure of the event, the pressure to write brilliant prose had been lifted. And in its place was the pleasure of learning by doing. Of taking risks, of making messes. Of following ideas just to see where they lead.

Writing for quantity rather than quality, I discovered, had the strange effect of bringing about both. It didn't necessarily make a whole lot of sense to me, especially as a writer who had spent days laboring over seventy-five-word record reviews for the local paper. But the proof was incontrovertible, and everyone who finished NaNoWriMo that first year agreed: We were only able to write so well—and have such a merry time doing it—because we wrote so quickly and intensely. The roar of adrenaline drowned out the self-critical voices that tend to make creative play such work for adults.

Lessons Learned →

I've taken part in National Novel Writing Month every year since 1999. Through the good books and bad, I've learned a lot about getting first drafts written, and picked up countless strategies, tips, and significant-other-annoying behaviors that help get that initial, breathless sketch of a novel down on paper.

I think the lasting insights from that first year, though, boil down to four revelations.

1. Enlightenment Is Overrated

Before being swept up in the momentum of National Novel Writing Month, my general approach to fiction writing was to stall as long as possible. In fact, I had high hopes of delaying any novel attempts until I was older and wiser, and had achieved a state of literary enlightenment.

If all went according to plan, this all-seeing wisdom would occur somewhere around my ninetieth birthday. And then, fully primed, I would simply dictate the Nobel Prize–worthy manuscript to my nursemaid, who would then pass it on to an appropriate publisher.

Having written a redeemable novel as a twenty-six-year-old made me realize that "sooner" definitely trumps "later" when it comes to writing. Every period in one's life, I saw, bustles with novel-worthy passions, dilemmas, and energies specific to that age. The novels I wrote in my twenties were much different from the ones I wrote in my thirties, which will be much different from the ones I will write in my sixties. What better reason to get writing now? With each passing era, a new novel is possible. And a potentially great book you could have written slips away.

2. Being Busy Is Good for Your Writing

You've probably heard the old adage that if you want to get something done, you should ask a busy person to do it. I've discovered this is acutely true when it comes to novel writing.

Because here's the thing: However attractive the idea of a writer's retreat may sound, having all day to poke around on a novel actually *hampers* productivity. This is something I suspected after the first year of NaNoWriMo, and something I confirmed after the second—when, emboldened by a pair of questionable successes in the month-long noveling field, I decided that the only thing separating me from the world's best-seller lists was three months of uninterrupted writing time.

And so I spent the following half year saving up enough money to resign my various obligations for three months, and then dove into the deliriously productive life of a full-time novelist.

Things went awry almost immediately. With nothing to do all day but write, I found myself doing everything *but* writing. Essential errands were run. Laundry was done. The bathroom was cleaned. Less essential errands were run. The bathroom was recleaned. A complex rooftop Habitrail system designed to make tree-to-tree transitioning easier for the neighborhood squirrels was built and nearly installed before the county's animal services unit intervened. And so on.

The mounting guilt I felt each evening over accomplishing so little writing during the day would then force me to cancel the plans I had made with friends that night. So I could stay in and get some writing done.

Night, of course, simply involved more work on the Habitrail.

At the end of the three months, I was frustrated, my friends were worried, and the squirrels continued to make their clumsy, desperate leaps from branch to branch. The experiment in nonstop writing was a total disaster.

For me the moral of the story is this: A rough draft is best written in the steam cooker of an already busy life. If you have a million things to do, adding item #1,000,001 is not such a big deal. When, on the other hand, you have nothing to do, getting out of bed and washing yourself before 2:00 p.m. feels like too much work to even contemplate.

As Isaac Newton observed, objects in motion tend to stay in motion. When writing your first draft, being busy is key. It may feel frustrating at first, but having daily writing periods curtailed by chores, family, and other distractions actually helps you get the thing done. This is partly because the hectic pace forces you to type with a fleet-fingered desperation. But it's mostly because noveling in the midst of a chaotic life makes "book time" a treat rather than an obligation. It's a small psychological shift, but it makes all the difference in the world.

3. Plot Happens

From that first NaNoWriMo, I learned that you are allowed to begin a novel simply by turning on the nearest computer and typing. You don't need to do research; you don't need to understand anything about your characters or plan out your setting. It's fine to just start. And making it up as you go along does not require you to be a particularly gifted novelist. That first year, I started with neither plot nor characters, and I ended up with a reasonably accomplished novel that had tension and momentum and even a subplot or two. And I did all that with an imagination the size of a pea.

If you spend enough time with your characters, plot simply happens. This makes novel writing, in essence, a literary trapeze act, one where you have to blindly trust that your imagination and intuition will be there to catch you and fling you onward at each stage of your high-flying journey.

The good news is that our imaginations live for these high-pressure situations. The human brain is an agile, sure-handed partner, an attention-loving, razzle-dazzle showthing that can pull plausible transitions out of thin air and catch us before anything (save our pride) gets too terribly injured on our inevitable tumbles.

The key to writing a novel is to realize that you are in the best hands possible: your own. Ray Bradbury said it best: "Your intuition knows what it wants to write, so get out of the way."

4. Writing for Its Own Sake Has Surprising Rewards

That first year I learned that writing a novel simply feels great. Slipping into "the zone"—that place where you become a passive conduit to a story—exercises your brain in cool ways and makes life a little bit more enchanted. No matter what your talent level, novel writing is a low-stress, high-rewards hobby.

After I'd written my own manuscript, I also found myself able to appreciate my favorite books on a different level. I stopped taking the text for granted and began noticing a host of crafty details and well-concealed seams. To really get behind the scenes and understand the books you love, it helps to write one yourself. Creating my own manuscript also opened my mind to the joys of genres I'd never read before, as I became curious about the way different kinds of books are put together.

And, finally, the more I wrote, the better my writing became. I now see each of the first drafts I've written as a thirty-day scholarship to the most exclusive, important writing academy in the world. If there's one thing successful novelists agree on, it's this: The single best thing you can do to improve your writing is to write. Copiously.

The more books you have under your belt, the more comfortable you are with your writing voice, and the more confident you are in your style. Treating a novel like a hands-on writing classroom—where advancement relies as much on dramatic failures as it does on heroic successes—has been an amazingly liberating experience for me. And it's taught me exactly which aspects of noveling I'm good at (drinking coffee and complaining) and what my weaknesses are (dialogue, character development, plot, etc.).

It's invaluable feedback, and I couldn't have gotten it any other way.

Meanwhile, Back at NaNoWriMo Headquarters →

And what happened to NaNoWriMo after that first year? In 2000, I moved National Novel Writing Month from July to November to more fully take advantage of the miserable weather. That second year, 140 people signed up, and 29 people ended up winning.

Then word began to spread about NaNoWriMo. The *Los Angeles Times* did an article, as did *USA Today*. A talented programmer built the new, more-robust NaNoWriMo.org site for the event, one with discussion boards, novel-excerpt posting areas, personalized word-count progress bars, and a winner verification system.

The event grew larger still—five thousand participants the third year—and I continued to work as both director and participant, sending out pep-talk emails, overseeing the website, and interacting with nascent NaNoWriMo chapters around the world.

Fast-forward to November 2014, and NaNoWriMo now produces over 3.5 billion words of fiction each year—more than all of America's creative writing programs combined.

Nearly two hundred participants have sold their creations to publishers, and nine *New York Times* best sellers have started out as NaNoWriMo manuscripts. Tens of thousands of our participants have self-published their books.

The biggest success stories in National Novel Writing Month, though, are usually the unpublished ones. These are the stories of everyday people who, over the course of one frantic month, discover that literature is not merely a spectator sport. Who learn that fiction writing can be a blast when you set aside your fears and dive headlong into the creative process.

Your Mission →

No Plot? No Problem! is intended as a guidebook and companion for that month-long vacation into the weird, wonderful realm of the imagination. In its nine chapters, I've tried to stuff years of accumulated novel-writing tips, tricks, strategies, and schemes, as well as dos, don'ts, and encouraging anecdotes from dozens of NaNoWriMo veterans.

Chapters 1 through 3 describe how to prepare for the actual writing month. They guide you in creating a realistic schedule and gathering the tools and treats that are essential in bashing out your book. They also look at ways to turn your home and immediate surroundings into phenomenally productive word factories, and lay out winning tactics to transform innocent bystanders into cheerleaders and fellow travelers on the journey.

Chapter 4 introduces such novelish concepts as plot, setting, and character, and helps you uncover what it is you'd actually like to write about during your upcoming writing marathon.

Chapters 5 through 8 serve as a week-by-week guide to your writing adventure. They lay out the issues and dilemmas particular to each week, and offer plenty of exercises for sparking your creativity, pep talks from published NaNoWriMo authors, and goofy ways to bag the day's word-count quota while maintaining inspired and generally coherent storytelling.

Chapter 9 offers some thoughts and advice on post-novel life, particularly on making a graceful transition back into the day-to-day world, and it also contains a guide to rewriting one-month novels for those interested in shaping, polishing, and publishing their work. *No Plot? No Problem!* makes a perfect companion for those looking to undertake the madcap National Novel Writing Month in November. But because November is an already-overloaded month for many people (students, I'm looking at you), *No Plot? No Problem!* was also created as a year-round personal trainer for anyone interested in embarking on their own month-long noveling journey.

Whether you plan on writing your novel in winter or summer, next week or next year, I hope you'll find in these pages the friendly kick in the pants needed to help you take your book from embryonic idea to completed draft in one action-packed month.

With great caffeinated well-wishes,

Chris Baty

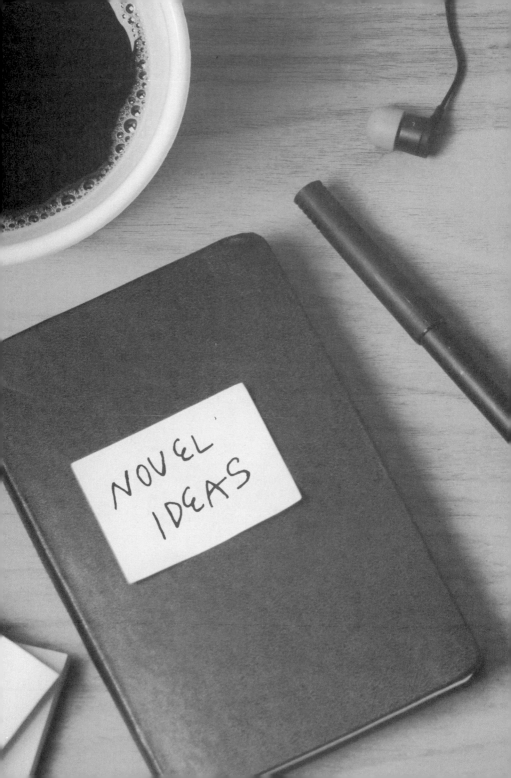

A ROUND-TRIP TICKET TO NOVEL-LAND:

Gearing Up for Your Writing Adventure!

1. SECRET WEAPONS, EXUBERANT IMPERFECTIONS, AND THE END OF THE "ONE DAY" NOVELIST

Once upon a time, I believed that you needed to have several things before you set out to write a novel. These were, in order of importance:

- ☑ Heart-fibrilating amounts of coffee
- ☑ Plot
- ☑ Character
- ☑ Setting

When I actually sat down to write my first novel back in 1999, though, I discovered that my ideas about novel writing were woefully mistaken. You *don't* need a plot before you write a novel, nor do you need an evocative sense of place or a winsome, engaging cast. You don't even need coffee (though I still haven't allowed myself to fully come to terms with that yet).

What you really need is a secret weapon.

You need a superpowered, diabolical device that will transform you into a bastion of literary accomplishment. And I'm happy to report that this implement is in the house, and it's just waiting for you to pick it up.

The Mystery Machine and You →

Without hyperbole, I can say that this tool (tucked securely at the end of this chapter) is the most awesome catalyst that has ever been unleashed on the worlds of art and commerce. Nearly every beautiful and useful thing you've ever touched or witnessed was born in its mighty forge. It's portable, affordable, and nonpolluting.

It's also invisible.

What you need to write a novel, of course, is a deadline.

Deadlines are the dynamos of the modern age. They've built every city, won every contest, and helped all of us pay our taxes reasonably close to on time for years and years. Deadlines bring focus, forcing us to make time for the achievements we would otherwise postpone, encouraging us to reach beyond our conservative estimates of what we think possible, helping us to wrench victory from the jaws of sleep.

A deadline is, simply put, optimism in its most ass-kicking form. It's a potent force that, when wielded with respect, will level any obstacle in its path. This is especially true when it comes to creative pursuits.

Because in the artistic realms, deadlines do much more than just get projects finished. They serve as creative midwives and enthusiastic shepherds adept at plucking the timid inspirations that lurk in the wings of our imaginations and flinging them bodily into the bright light of day. The bigger the artistic project, the more it needs a deadline to keep marshaling those shy ideas out onto the world's stage.

Nowhere is this more true than in novel writing, when even people who know what they're doing have trouble getting the things finished. Drafting a novel typically involves years of navigating a jungle of plots, subplots, supporting characters, tangents, symbols, and motifs. It's an exhilarating trek at times, but it also involves long, long slogs, where chapters are built, dismantled, and rebuilt dozens of times. A single troublesome passage may stop the writing for years as the writer fusses and stews and waits for the way forward to become clear.

Writing on deadline changes that. Having an end date for your quest through the noveling unknown is like bringing along a team of jetpack-wearing, entrepreneurial Sherpas. These energetic guides not only make passage easier through myriad formidable obstacles, but they'll fly ahead and open coffee shops and convenience stores along the route.

A Good Deadline Is Hard to Find

The problem, as those of us who are forever grumbling about our uncreative lives know, is that rock-solid, dream-fostering deadlines are hard to come by in the arts world. It's a sad irony that deadlines are given so freely at work (where we want them least), and are in such short supply in the extracurricular activities where we need them most.

INSPIRING TALES OF HIGH-SPEED MAYHEM

Caffeine and literature have long enjoyed a very productive relationship. Some high-speed books you might have read include Anne Rice's *Interview with a Vampire* (five weeks, for a contest deadline), William Faulkner's *As I Lay Dying* (six weeks), Robert Louis Stevenson's *The Strange Case of Dr. Jekyll and Mr. Hyde* (three days), Chuck Palahniuk's *Fight Club* (two weeks), and the first book in the Perry Mason series, which creator Erle Stanley Gardner dictated in just four days (while working half days at his law practice, no less!).

THIS DANGEROUS BLOODSPORT CALLED NOVEL WRITING

If you've spent any amount of time using a computer, you already know the range of sneaky ways they have of wrecking your body. Carpal tunnel syndrome, eye strain, back problems, numb-butt . . . the list of computer-inspired woes goes on and on.

Because you'll likely be racking up an extraordinary amount of typing time when you write your novel, you are going to be putting your body at high risk for damage. This is no joke: Take it easy on yourself by setting up an ergonomic writing station, taking stretch breaks, and calling it a night at the first sign of numbness. Google tips on posture and keyboard placement, and keep eyedrops on hand to ward off the inevitable dryness that comes from getting so wrapped up in your book that you forget to blink (a great sign for your story, but a not-so-great sign for your poor eyeballs).

Outside of writing classes, we never quite get the professional-grade push we need to tackle big, juicy, creative projects like novel writing. And who has time for classes? We're slammed at work and busy at home. Throw in an occasional outing with friends or significant others, and we're ready for bed at 10:00 p.m. every night. *Really* ready for bed. There's barely enough time in a day to cover all our mandatory obligations, so optional activities like novel writing, journaling, painting, or playing music—things that feel great but that no one will ever take us to task for shirking—are invariably left for another day.

Which is how most of us become "one day" novelists. As in, "One day, I'd really like to write a novel." The problem is that that day never seems to come, and so we're stuck. Or we *were* stuck, anyway. Because as far as artistic deadlines go, this book comes with a doozy.

The deadline that rules over this book with an iron fist is the ink-sensitive model #A30/31/50k. Once activated, it gives you just one month to write a 50,000-word rough draft of a novel. Plus, it hounds you every step of the way, forcing you to write when you don't want to, badgering you into meeting daily word-count goals, and turning your life into an obsessive literary hell for four weeks.

The #A30/31/50k will also foster one of the most intense and satisfying months of your life. In the thirty or thirty-one days you spend under its taskmastering thumb, you'll discover wild parts of yourself and tap into realms of aptitude and achievement you didn't know existed. You'll fly and soar and laugh and sing, and the people who love you most will likely worry that you've gone crazy.

That's okay. The insanity only lasts a month—just long enough to get "write a novel" checked off your to-do list. And then normal life, with its regular showers and reasonably clean apartments, can begin again. Should you decide to take your month-long novel and revise it to perfection later, you can do that. If not, you'll still have experienced a creative month like no other.

Okay, One Month Sounds Good. But Why 50,000 Words? →

I'd like to say that NaNoWriMo's 50,000-word threshold was achieved by a scientific assessment of the great short novels of our age. The real story is that when I started this whole month-long-noveling escapade, I simply grabbed the shortest novel on my shelf—which happened to be Aldous Huxley's *Brave New World*—did a rough word count of it, and went with that figure.

Over the years, though, 50,000 words has proven itself a good goal for a month's labors. Writing 50,000 words in a month breaks down to about 1,667 words per day. Most average typists will be able to dispatch that in an hour and a half, which makes it doable, even for people with full-time jobs and chaotic home lives. Fifty thousand words is also just large enough for someone writing concisely to sketch an entire story arc within its borders.

And yet, despite its short stature, a 50,000-word novel is no cake-walk. Only about 17 percent of National Novel Writing Month partic-ipants reach the 50,000-word finish line every year, and some have argued that the number should be lowered.

I think the number is perfect. Because you're covering so much ground, so quickly, the high number forces you to lower your expecta-tions for your prose, to write for quantity over quality, and to stop being so hard on yourself. And this, for a first draft, is the pathway to genius.

Low Expectations, High Yield →

If your fiction is anything like mine, you have long since become accustomed to the concept of underachievement. Celebrating your writing inadequacies, though, will likely be a new and somewhat uncomfortable prospect. Give it a try when you write your novel next month. The most important mental preparation you can do for the noveling month ahead is to realize the following: There is no pres-sure on you to write a brilliant first draft. Because no one ever writes a brilliant first draft.

It's true. When your novel first peeks its head into the world, it will look pretty much like every newborn: blotchy, hairless, and utterly confused. This is the case no matter how talented you are, or how long you take to coax the thing into existence. Novels are sim-ply too long and complex to nail on the first go-round. Anyone who tells you differently is a superhuman literary cyborg, and should not be trusted.

I'm not making this up. Flip through books on writing by Stephen King or Anne Lamott, and they say the same thing (without, of course, the crucial insights on cyborgs). To quote the mild-mannered, word-mincing Ernest Hemingway: "The first draft of anything is shit."

It's not just shit, though. It's *wonderful* shit. A first draft is an anything-goes space for you to roll up your sleeves and make a terrific mess. It is a place where the writer's battle plan is redrawn daily; a place where recklessness and risk-taking is rewarded, where half-assed planning and tangential writing can yield unexpectedly amazing results. It is, in short, a place for people like you and me.

And when it comes to the topsy-turvy world of the rough draft, the law of the land is best summed up in two words: exuberant imperfection.

Exuberant Imperfection Defined

The first law of exuberant imperfection is essentially this: The quickest, easiest way to produce something beautiful and lasting is to risk making something horribly crappy.

Like most things associated with writing a novel in a month, this may not make a lot of sense on the surface. But there's proven psychology behind it. Namely, the older we get, the more scared we are to try new things. Especially things that might make us look stupid in public. (Women with boyfriends or husbands can see this in action by suggesting they take salsa dancing classes together.)

The reason for this is that, as grown-ups, we come to place undue importance on this thing called "competence." From the work world, we've learned that the way to get ahead in life is to brandish proficiency and know-how at anything that moves—coworkers, bosses, customers, and so on. We do this for a very good reason: to keep from getting fired.

In the workplace, the emphasis on professionalism makes great sense. No one wants to have his or her cerebellum doctored by a dilettante brain surgeon. But the emphasis on mastery has certain unseen psychological ramifications on the rest of our lives. You'd think, for instance, that this workaday obsession with competence would make our weekends a refuge for floundering forays into uncharted territories.

But what do we do when we have free time? The tried-and-true activities we've already perfected. Like texting. Or walking up and down stairs. Or getting drunk. The times we do actually make a point of stepping out of our normal routine, we tend to get flustered when we don't get the hang of it right away. This is especially true with artistic endeavors. At the first awkward line of prose or botched brushstroke, we hurriedly pack away the art supplies and scamper back to our domains of proficiency. Better a quitter than a failure, our subconscious reasoning goes.

Exuberant imperfection allows you to circumvent those limiting feelings entirely. It dictates that the best way to tackle daunting, paralysis-inducing challenges is to give yourself permission to make mistakes, and then go ahead and make them.

In the context of novel writing, this means you should lower the bar from "best-seller" to "would not make someone vomit." Exuberant imperfection encourages you to write uncritically, to experiment, to break your time-honored rules of writing just to see what happens. In a first draft, nothing is permanent, and everything is fixable. So stay loose and flexible, and keep your expectations very, very low.

It sounds like a recipe for a disastrous novel, I know. But as you'll discover when you start writing, lowered expectations don't necessarily translate into lowered quality. Exuberant imperfection

ISN'T 50,000 WORDS MORE OF A NOVELLA?

While it's true that 50,000 words makes for a short novel, it does not make what you are about to write a novella.

Novellas, as decreed by the Global Council on Literary Weights and Measurements in its precedent-setting 1956 ruling, are "weak-willed, half-hearted novels" that "lack the gumption to make it to 50,000 words," which they very accurately describe as "the very precipice of novelhood."

But mainly the reason to avoid describing your upcoming work as a novella is that it doesn't impress people the way *novel* does. Remember: You're writing a novel next month. Don't let anyone tell you different.

is not a surefire path to bad writing so much as it is a necessary mental reshuffling, a psychological sleight-of-hand that takes the pressure off and helps you tolerate the drivel that greases the wheels of genius. In your first draft, the ratio of muck to mastery may be somewhat disappointing. But that's just life as a draft-wranglin' novelist. It will all get better in time. For now, quantity—not quality—is of primary importance.

And embracing exuberant imperfection will do much more than just help keep your word counts soaring in the coming month. By giving yourself the gift of imperfection, you tap into the realms of intuition and imagination that your hypercritical brain normally censors. These are the left-of-center dialogue exchanges and strange character quirks that end up forming the most memorable and delightful parts of your novel.

This torrent of thoughts and ideas is exhilarating and scary, and absolutely, absolutely essential to getting a first draft written in such a short amount of time.

Writing in Packs →

Along with a rigid, rigorous deadline and an anything-goes writing approach, there is one more prerequisite for pulling a surprisingly competent book out of yourself quickly: finding company.

Ideally, you will find people interested in taking the noveling plunge alongside you, cranking out their own questionable masterworks in the same month you do. But "company" can also simply mean finding nonwriting friends and loved ones who agree to check in on your progress throughout the month, providing a little friendly support along the way.

If you've been writing fiction for a while, you may already be a member of a writing group. The typical writing group, however, is actually a *reading* group; it's there to give feedback on works each member produces in isolation. The group you want to form now is one where you meet up to actually write. No sharing. No critiques. No feedback whatsoever. Just pure, unadulterated output.

For most people (and I used to count myself among them), writing is a private act, and the thought of writing en masse sounds both terrifying and highly unproductive. Give it a shot. You'd be surprised how much the clack of other people typing brings out the novelist beast in you, and how much the push of friendly competition will keep you working on your story even when you're ready to kill all of your characters.

Activating Your Deadline →

Before you can let everyone know that you're writing a novel in a month, you first need to square it with yourself. So go get that calendar and pick out the best month to do this. No month is going to be perfect, but here are some signs of a good one: abysmal weather, a built-in three-day weekend, and the chance that your family or housemates might accidentally be beamed to another galaxy for thirty days.

Barring that, all months are pretty much equal. The one bit of advice I do offer in choosing your time frame is to write over the course of a calendar month, rather than simply picking thirty-one consecutive days. Structure and drama are both essential in the coming endeavor, and both will be heightened if your deadline coincides with a month's end.

Once you've picked your month, just read and sign the *No Plot? No Problem!* "Month-Long Novelist Agreement and Statement of Understanding (Form #A30/31/50k)." Then post a photo of the signed document on the social media site of your choice and meet me at Chapter 2. We have some planning to do.

WHAT DOES 50,000 WORDS LOOK LIKE?

The book you're holding in your hands is just north of 50,000 words. Some other books checking in at around 50,000 words include:

The Absolutely True Diary of a Part-Time Indian
by Sherman Alexie

Brave New World
by Aldous Huxley

Ethan Frome
by Edith Wharton

Fahrenheit 451
by Ray Bradbury

Generation X
by Douglas Coupland

The Giver
by Lois Lowry

The Great Gatsby
by F. Scott Fitzgerald

The Hitchhiker's Guide to the Galaxy
by Douglas Adams

Lord of the Flies
by William Golding

The Ocean at the End of the Lane
by Neil Gaiman

The Outsiders
by S.E. Hinton

Slaughterhouse-Five
by Kurt Vonnegut

However, keep in mind that the 50,000-word rough draft you write next month will likely balloon out by 10,000 to 50,000 words in a rewrite. The typical paperback you see on a bookstore shelf is about 100,000 words, with shorter genre fiction, like serial romances or sci-fi tie-ins, coming in at 50,000 to 70,000 words.

THE MONTH-LONG **NOVELIST AGREEMENT** AND STATEMENT OF UNDERSTANDING

I hereby pledge my intent to write a 50,000-word novel in one month's time. By invoking an absurd, month-long deadline on such an enormous undertaking, I understand that notions of "craft," "brilliance," and "competency" are to be chucked right out the window, where they will remain, ignored, until they are retrieved for the editing process. I understand that I am a talented person, capable of heroic acts of creativity, and I will give myself enough time over the course of the next month to allow my innate gifts to come to the surface, unmolested by self-doubt, self-criticism, and other acts of self-bullying.

During the month ahead, I realize I will produce clunky dialogue, clichéd characters, and deeply flawed plots. I agree that all of these things will be left in my rough draft, to be corrected and/or excised at a later point. I understand my right to withhold my manuscript from all readers until I deem it completed. I also acknowledge my right as author to substantially inflate both the quality of the rough draft and the rigors of the writing process should such inflation prove useful in garnering me respect and attention, or freedom from participation in onerous household chores.

I acknowledge that the month-long, 50,000-word deadline I set for myself is absolute and unchangeable, and that any failure to meet the deadline, or any effort on my part to move the deadline once the adventure has begun, will invite well-deserved mockery from friends and family. I also acknowledge that, upon successful completion of the stated noveling objective, I am entitled to a period of gleeful celebration and revelry, the duration and intensity of which may preclude me from participating fully in workplace activities for days, if not weeks, afterward.

_____   _____
SIGNED   DATE

_____   _____
NOVEL START DATE   NOVEL DEADLINE

2. TIME-FINDING, NEWS-BREAKING, AND A STEP-BY-STEP GUIDE TO TRANSFORMING LOVED ONES INTO EFFECTIVE AGENTS OF GUILT AND TERROR

Tim Lohnes was in pain. The cartographer from Oakland, California, was less than a week into NaNoWriMo, and his story was floundering.

"I just didn't know what to do with my characters," he says. "Plus, my wrists were hurting, and I had three work projects that were keeping me up until 2:00 a.m. every night."

Tim tried to resurrect the story in the second week, managing to get his word count up to 12,000. But it just wasn't happening, and that's when Tim stopped working on the book entirely.

Then, with three days left in the writing month, Tim got a new idea for his book. "I just started feeling it," he says.

Tim dove into his tale for a third time. And this time it caught. Tim raced against time, sleeping five hours a night, pounding out 38,000 words in three days, typing "The End" at the 50,006-word mark. There were fifteen minutes left to go on the month's clock.

All of this would be utterly extraordinary if Tim didn't do it this way every year. Yep. In five years of doing NaNoWriMo, Tim has always written most of his book, and become a winner every time, at the last minute. And he's not alone. Every NaNoWriMo, tens of thousands of writers leap from four-digit word counts to the 50,000-word finish line in the final few days of the contest.

Tim—and the other writers who have learned to turn procrastination into performance art—would be the first to admit that writing an entire manuscript in three days exacts a high toll on your book and your body. But their exploits underline an important fact of this whole endeavor: Writing 50,000 words of fiction really doesn't take that much time. Slow writers find they can write about 800 words of novel per hour; a speedy writer (and good typist) can easily do twice that. Which means that the whole novel draft, from start to finish, will take most folks about fifty-five hours.

If you had the luxury of writing eight hours a day, seven days a week, you could begin on a Monday morning and be wrapping up your epilogue in time for brunch on Sunday.

Few of us, though, can write eight hours a day, seven days a week. In fact, between school, jobs, and the host of other daily events that fill our lives, carving fifty-five hours of quiet time, however small that number looks on paper, ends up being quite a challenge.

Enter the

TIME FINDER.

Finding Your Forgo-able with the Time Finder →

The Time Finder is to novel planning what the Jaws of Life is to accident scenes. But rather than extracting precious things from tight places, the Time Finder does the opposite: It helps wedge large valuables into impossibly small spaces. The tool is the ideal way to discover the answer to the inevitable question, "Where the hell am I going to find time to write a novel?"

To use it, you only need some paper, a pen, and some red, blue, and green highlighters (or colored pencils). You'll also need five minutes a night for seven nights in a row. And before you start complaining about getting homework already, let it be known: There are treats involved.

Here's how it works: Before you go to bed every night, sit down with your paper and pen and write down everything you did that day. Start with the moment you woke up and carry it through to the time you turned on the Time Finder. For me, yesterday's list looked like this:

☑ **7:30–8:00** Made and consumed breakfast.

☑ **8:00–8:30** Showered, brushed teeth, got dressed. Lay back-down in bed. Reluctantly got back up again.

☑ **8:30–10:00** Emailed friends and killed time online.

☑ **10:00–1:30** Actually worked.

☑ **1:30–2:30** Lunch. More internet.

☑ **2:30–5:00** Worked some more.

☑ **5:00–5:30** Drove to the post office. Returned.

☑ **5:30–6:00** Read *The Onion* and watched dumb videos.

☑ **6:00–6:30** Email.

☑ **6:30–7:00** Talked on the phone, considered cleaning the apartment.

☑ **7:00–7:30** Went for a short walk.

☑ **7:30–8:30** Went out to dinner with girlfriend (note to self: never again eat a deep-fried anything that's referred to as an"awesome blossom").

☑ **8:30–9:30** Took a stab at actually cleaning up apartment, halfheartedly washed some dishes, called parents.

☑ **9:30–10:00** Hastily assembled package I was supposed to send for Mom's birthday two weeks ago.

☑ **10:00–10:15** Paid bills.

☑ **10:15–11:00** Worked some more.

☑ **11:00–12:00** Read.

☑ **12:00** Activated Time Finder.

After you've finished each daily log, reward yourself with a delicious, nonnutritious treat, and then go to sleep. (Sleep, by the way, should not be included on the Time Finder's list of items, as hoarding as much sleep as possible every night is the birthright of writers everywhere.)

After you've carefully documented your activities for one week, bust out the highlighters or colored pencils, and go to town. First, circle or underline every REQUIRED activity in red. These are the top-tier items that you have to do every day or risk unemployment, eviction, expulsion, or mental collapse. Things in this category would be basic acts of personal hygiene, commutes to work or school, actual working, running work-related errands, eating meals, shuttling family around, grocery shopping, and paying bills.

Next, go through the lists and mark the HIGHLY DESIRED activities in blue. In this category go the things that, if push came to shove, you could get by without doing for a month, but which would cause major stress or hardship. This second tier of activities could include exercising, returning social phone calls and emails, keeping up with the news, attending birthday parties, or going to professional or religious get-togethers.

Finally, take that last color and mark all the FORGO-ABLE activities that you could give up for a month without courting disaster. This includes Facebook trawling, online shopping, TV watching, making art, nonessential home repairs, hobby-based tinkering, and recreational reading.

Okay, now it's time to shift the Time Finder into overdrive. Go through the forgo-able items and add up how many hours you spend per day, on average, in their pursuit. As you can see from my list, I tend to spend about three hours every day doing things that I could sacrifice for thirty days without my life falling apart.

If, like me, you've found that you're spending between an hour and a half to two hours a day on forgo-able items, you're golden. These will be your sacrificial lambs next month. Say good-bye to them now, and know they will still be there when you pick them up again in thirty days.

When I'm writing a novel, I stop internet surfing entirely, limit my leisure reading, and spend much less weeknight time with (non-noveling) friends. Other writers use the opportunity to pare back conversations with their in-laws and stop doing yard work. The choice is yours; all you need to do is find an hour and a half or so per day in the forgo-able category and you've got a green light to write.

If you can't trim the fat you need from the forgo-able items, you'll need to slice into the meat of your highly desired activities. Because these are more important, the best approach is to cut down on frequency rather than eliminate them entirely. Plan on skipping a meeting or two, duck out of birthday parties a little early, and make your child hitchhike home from school a couple of days a week.

If you find yourself dipping into the "required" category to come up with the hours you need to write, congratulations. You are in the top 1 percent of busy people everywhere. The good news about this is that you've only survived this long by multitasking at an Olympic level. You'll be able to bring all those keen time-management skills to bear on your novel. If you haven't had a heart attack yet, odds are good you probably won't next month either.

THE GOLDEN RULE OF SCHEDULING

Though every productive noveling schedule is unique, and what works for one frantic writer won't necessarily work for another, there is one golden rule you should keep in mind when laying out your writing schedule: Don't take more than two nights off from your novel in a row.

Taking a three-day vacation from your book will not only stall whatever momentum you've developed in the story, it will also give your brain too much time to come up with doubts and other foot-dragging assessments of your work. In the same way cults tend to keep recent converts inside the compound walls, so should you make sure your brain doesn't go AWOL for too long from your novel.

Let's assume, though, that you, like most people, can get ten to fourteen hours a week through some basic leisure-time restrictions. If that's the case, leave everything else in your life alone. It may be tempting to use the novel as a cornerstone for a total lifestyle overhaul, but this is a decidedly bad time to implement ambitious changes in your life.

In fact, the best thing you can do for yourself, your manuscript, and those around you is to keep as many of your old routines as possible. Being available for some social activities helps keep your mind fresh for the book, and also forestalls mutiny among your friends and family.

Scheduling Your Writing Time →

Which brings us to the important question: How to allocate the soon-to-be-liberated hours the Time Finder just uncovered? Pacing is obviously important, but what is a good pace? Should you write every day? Every other day? On weekdays only? Does the onset of a bad mood mean you get to skip a planned writing session? What about an exploding pancreas?

Unfortunately, there are no hard-and-fast answers to any of these questions (save the case of exploding body parts, which warrants a one-day writing exemption). Even professional novelists have wildly conflicting theories about the ideal times and durations for writing sessions.

The chief tactic in formulating a winning battle plan for your noveling schedule is to try a variety of approaches early on, discover what works best for you, and use it relentlessly thereafter.

My personal technique is to write for two hours per night, three or four nights per week. I pair that with three separate one-hour sessions on either Saturday or Sunday.

Why do I do this? Habit. And because it seems to work. It also gives me one or two weeknights and one entire weekend day away from my book. This makes it exponentially less likely that I'll kill myself or those around me, and I still tend to arrive at the 50,000-word point a couple of days before the month ends.

Some NaNoWriMo participants do all of their writing in the morning before work, taking advantage of the relative quiet of the predawn hours. Still others make a point of nabbing half of the day's word-count quota on their lunch break, and typing out the rest on their train ride home.

We'll get into the pros and cons of various noveling locations in Chapter 3. For now, the best way to approach your scheduling is with a light heart and an open mind. Because inevitably, over the course of the month, you'll encounter a variety of emergencies that will curtail your chapters and muffle your muse. Friends will pick your noveling month to have relationship meltdowns. Your three favorite bands will come to town on the one night you'd set aside to finally get caught up on your word count. And your computer, which has worked flawlessly for the past five years, will explode in an apocalyptic series of error screens.

When this happens, just go with it. Sometimes taking a night off to go to that show is the best thing you can do for your novel. And other times, you'll need to ask your friends to nail two-by-fours across your study door to make sure you have no way of fleeing your writing responsibilities. Having a ready supply of concert tickets and three-inch nails on hand, depending on your progress and mood, is the surest path to scheduling success.

Hope for the Best, Plan for the Worst

Even with all the vagaries of the novel-writing process, there are a few problems you can anticipate. Week One, for instance, is much easier than Week Two. It's a good idea to set aside a little extra time in the first seven days to rack up as many words as possible before the going gets tough.

Other predictable problems vary depending on personality. I, for one, am an inveterate procrastinator. While I regale my friends every year with the same wild-eyed promises about getting way ahead of my word-count quota early and staying far out in front of the writing pack the whole month, in truth I'm always struggling a little toward the end to finish the book on time.

NOVELING THROUGH THE SPACE-TIME CONTINUUM: THE NANOWRIMO TEMPORAL VORTEX

In my forays into month-long noveling, I've repeatedly noticed something that seems, on the surface, impossible. Which is this: When I introduce novel writing into my schedule, I actually seem to have more time for running errands and goofing off. Other NaNoWriMo participants have confirmed the phenomenon, which seems to stem from a short-term willingness to maximize every minute of the day to startlingly productive effect. A side effect of this is that the moments you do choose to spend on leisure activities become imbued with a sort of Technicolor radiance, with everyday pleasures like unhurried conversations or book reading taking on an unbelievable lushness. Strange, but true.

Because of my steadfast, rock-solid procrastinating ways, I've learned to keep the entire final week and weekend of the month free of social obligations. I make sure any out-of-town trips happen in the beginning or middle of the month. I also do my best to reduce my workload (or, ahem, fall deathly ill) on the final Thursday and Friday of the event. Usually, I don't need all the time I set aside for myself, but the few times when eye strain or wrist problems have slowed my typing toward the end of the month, having those extra hours available has been priceless.

Yes, there is something a little defeatist about accepting one's slacking ways rather than trying to fix them. That's a worry, though, for another month. The healthiest, most productive approach to writing is to acknowledge your weak spots early on, and build a writing plan that plays to your strengths and works around your liabilities.

Once you have your plan in place, you're ready to move on to the next important step: finding a support network for encouragement and companionship on your upcoming voyage.

Rallying the Troops →

For Trena Taylor, the decision to write a novel in a month didn't net her quite the outpourings of support she'd hoped.

"The announcement was greeted by a steady stream of blinking," the three-time NaNoWriMo winner from London says. "Total incomprehension. Most people just couldn't get 'round the idea that someone might actually want to write a novel, never mind the time frame. Why spend a month writing a book when it only takes five minutes to buy one from the shops, was the general attitude."

Ah, friends and family. The compassionate souls who will be your cheerleaders and voices of reason; the ones who will pick you up off the floor and set you gently back at the computer keyboard. And also the ones who are most likely to poke merciless fun at this ambitious, artistic plan you've dragged home.

Whether those closest to you love or hate the idea of you spending a month slaving over a novel, it's essential that they know about your plans. In the same way you wouldn't think about going on a long trip without checking in with your loved ones, you should make sure you brief everyone about your literary agenda.

Why? Because for all their potential helpfulness, your intimates can also make your thirty days in Novel-land very, very difficult. They can take your newfound shut-in tendencies personally, erode your willpower through succulent diversions, or demand extra amounts of your time just when you need it most for the book.

Mostly, though, you should talk to them because they are probably harboring secret noveling urges as well. And nothing diminishes the pain of extraordinary labors like having a friendly someone toiling there alongside you.

The Joys of Writing Companions

Novel writing is the perfect social activity. Granted, it is a social activity where no one is allowed to talk. And one where much of the pre- and post-event socializing consists of tearful laments about the deplorable state of one's writing and the meagerness of one's talents.

Maybe I have a strange idea of social activities, but this to me is heaven.

And a productive heaven at that. Writing with a partner (or three or four) helps all parties tap into the pool of competitive energy that forms when several people are working toward the same goal. When noveling with someone else, you have a pacer, a motivator, and a sympathetic ear for sharing the triumphs and tragedies of your novel. It's more productive and *a lot* more fun.

As you mull potential writing buddies, consider recruiting someone from the following groups:

Family Members • There's no surer way to guarantee a productive month than challenging a family member to a 50,000-word write-off. Siblings, especially, would rather die than let a brother

DOING THE NUMBERS: WHERE YOU SHOULD BE ON EACH DAY OF THE WORD PARADE

We'll do the worst-case-scenario math, and assume you're writing your novel in a thirty-day month.

DAY 1: 1,667 words

DAY 2: 3,334 words

DAY 3: 5,001 words

DAY 4: 6,668 words

DAY 5: 8,335 words

DAY 6: 10,002 words

DAY 7: 11,669 words

DAY 8: 13,336 words

DAY 9: 15,003 words

DAY 10: 16,670 words

DAY 11: 18,337 words

DAY 12: 20,004 words

DAY 13: 21,671 words

DAY 14: 23,338 words

DAY 15: 25,005 words

DAY 16: 26,672 words

DAY 17: 28,339 words

DAY 18: 30,006 words

DAY 19: 31,673 words

DAY 20: 33,340 words

DAY 21: 35,007 words

DAY 22: 36,674 words

DAY 23: 38,341 words

DAY 24: 40,008 words

DAY 25: 41,675 words

DAY 26: 43,342 words

DAY 27: 45,009 words

DAY 28: 46,676 words

DAY 29: 48,343 words

DAY 30: 50,000 words

or sister show them up, making novel completion a fait accompli for both parties. Kids and teens can also make excellent writing companions—see the Raising Your Own Noveling Army box for tips on bringing younger family members into the noveling fold.

The Up-for-Anything • These are the enthusiastic souls who savor the excitement of doing new things, regardless of the activity.

UFAs probably haven't done much writing, but they're excited by the challenge, and their congenitally low stress levels make them great companions.

The Creative Yearner • The CY grew up drawing, painting, writing, and playing music. In the past few years, though, the demands of daily life have forced these dreamers to put away their art supplies. The month of ferocious noveling will be a structured opportunity for them to get their creative juices flowing again.

The Corked Writer • A close cousin to the CY, the CW used to write a ton but stopped when something blocked the word well. Thirty-day novels have a way of blasting right through obstructions, and the contact high from being nearby when that happens is unforgettable.

Your Book Group • One of the great side effects of writing a novel is the deepened understanding it brings to books you read, making it an ideal activity for book groups. If you're in a reading group, propose that instead of tackling someone else's story next month, you each write your own. Then meet every week during the month to commiserate and celebrate your progress. When it's over, each member can bring his or her favorite passage to share.

And remember: If no one in your immediate area is up for the challenge, pitch the ideas to friends and relatives in faraway towns. Or look for writing buddies on the NaNoWriMo message boards. You may not be able to novel in the same space, but you can work together on video chat or have nightly word-count check-ins via text or email.

Filling the Home Team Bleachers

Just because someone declines the opportunity to come along on the writing journey doesn't mean that he or she can't be an essential part of the trip.

From cooking you the occasional dinner to checking in on your progress and mental stability, your support network of nonwriting friends will be invaluable in helping you survive the noveling slog. Because these are also the people most likely to be affected by your writing-inspired mood swings, your possible shortages of free time, and your substantially diminished regard for cleanliness ("I'll shower tomorrow, honey, I *promise!*"), it's a good idea to make sure they are on board.

When making my pitch for support to my loved ones every year, I always touch on the following four talking points:

Talking Point 1: It's not so much that I'll be totally absent for one month as it is that I'll be exceptionally present for the other eleven. • Amateur writers who take years and years to write their rough drafts are sentencing themselves and those around them to a constant barrage of "novel guilt." This is the hand-wringing, esteem-squishing sense of constant self-disappointment that accompanies any project that doesn't get worked on as often it should. By writing your entire rough draft in a month, you are not so much taking yourself out of your loved ones' lives for weeks as you are giving yourself to them for the years and years to come. By compressing all the procrastination and ensuing self-loathing into thirty manageable days, you'll be more pleasant to be around the rest of the time. (Don't mention the word "rewrite" until much, much later.)

Talking Point 2: I'll still have time for fun stuff while I work on my novel. • With all the pressure of cranking out a book-length work of fiction in such a short amount of time, you will be in need of fun, reviving distractions at various points throughout the month. And you'll have more time for socializing than you, or they, think. By removing the forgo-able items from your schedule, you'll likely have a few goofing-off hours per week that didn't exist before. You'll be busy, yes, but not *that* busy.

Talking Point 3: Doing this is important to me. • Those closest to us are also the ones who have heard all of our earnestly proclaimed, unfulfilled New Year's resolutions about gym-going, healthier eating, and other unrealistic pursuits. Your best friends are also the most likely to see this novel-in-a-month plan as another of your charmingly crackpot self-improvement schemes. Don't be offended if you encounter some good-natured ribbing; the idea of writing a novel in a month deserves to be laughed at. When the chuckles die down, though, do your best to make it clear that, however ridiculous the whole escapade may sound, you plan on seeing it through to completion. Also make it clear that when you are a best-selling author you will use a portion of your vast fortune to reward your supporters and destroy those who scoffed at you.

Talking Point 4: I need your help. • Everyone loves helping an underdog triumph against insurmountable odds. Talk to your best friends about all the obligations and chores you'll be juggling while you write, and have them brainstorm possible solutions and time-savers. You'll likely find a plethora of volunteers ready to help you get the small things accomplished so you'll have more time to go toe-to-toe with that literary Goliath.

Turning Close Friends into Obligations →

Gentle encouragement from your friends and family, however, is just the start. Warm smiles and you-can-do-it emails won't help you keep your butt in the chair when you're ready to give up in the middle of Week Two. After collecting a group of cheerleaders, the next step is to leverage all their goodwill into usable quantities of fear.

Yep. Terror is the amateur novelist's best friend. Without some amount of it pushing you onward toward your goal, you're going to lose momentum and quit. There are just too many other, more sensible things to do with your time than try to write a novel in a month, and all of these more interesting alternatives will become irresistible if you don't have some fear binding you to your word-processing device.

Happily, with a little work, your friends and family can terrify you in ways you'd never imagined.

Bragging as a Tool for Self-Motivation

When inculcating a healthy amount of fear, bragging is an indispensable tool. Nothing makes it more difficult to back down from a task than having boasted about it, in great detail, to all of your friends and loved ones. Think about it: Do you really want to be the butt of jokes *every* time novels are mentioned? For the *rest of your life*? Or have to hear your mother sigh when she learns that you have botched yet another attempt at making something of yourself?

I don't either. Which is why I make a point of laying a solid foundation of bragging way before I've thought about plot or setting or character. My ultimate goal is to back myself so far into a corner before the month even starts that I have no choice but to stay on course with the word count, no matter how dismally off track my novel gets in the weeks that follow.

RISKY BUSINESS: COMING CLEAN TO COWORKERS ABOUT YOUR NOVEL

Some month-long novelists have found some of their most vocal supporters among coworkers. But unless you work for an incredibly understanding company or have very close friends at work, I'd recommend not mentioning your project to fellow employees. Superman was Clark Kent to his coworkers, and you might want to be similarly discreet about your new superhero novel-writing powers around office mates. Not because they won't be encouraging, but because word about your efforts will inevitably make it back to your boss, who will then know exactly who to come to when someone prints multiple copies of a two-hundred-page document on the office printer at the end of the month.

In this way, bragging is an essential device for creating expectations. Not for genius prose, mind you. No, what you want to do is set up expectations for *completion*. For staying on track. For seeing it through to 50,000 words.

Some people pay personal trainers thousands of dollars to receive this sort of ongoing, disappointment-based motivation. Smart people get it from friends and family for free. Begin talking about your imminent ascent of the noveling ladder immediately after you have those first discussions with your friends about the thirty-day plunge.

In our wired age, email and social media are the most efficient paths to acquiring mass motivation. Send out boasting emails about your quest to everyone you know. Look up long-lost classmates on Facebook to inform them you will be a novelist in a couple of months. If you have a novel-friendly office, spam your department with your good writing news. This kind of outreach nets you, the writer, two invaluable things:

☑ 1. Constant motivational/envious/resentful check-ins from friends throughout the month about how the novel is going.

☑ 2. An irresistible invitation to widespread mockery should you not actually reach 50,000 words.

Betting the Bank

Lustily bragging about your upcoming noveling exploits often segues beautifully into the next recommended prewriting strategy: leveling huge, possibly crippling debts against the outcome of your novel.

For Andrew Johnson of Auckland, New Zealand, the opportunity came at the office.

"A disbelieving workmate challenged me when I said, 'I bet I can do it,'" recalls the ten-time NaNoWriMo winner.

"'Okay,' I said. 'How much?' I took fifty-dollar bets from any person willing to stake their cash on me being unable to complete the novel."

Andrew finished out the month with a new novel and a little extra pocket money. Unfortunately, he had to retire the scheme soon thereafter.

HOW TO HOST RUTHLESSLY PRODUCTIVE GROUP-WRITING EVENTS

If you don't have a laptop or tablet that allows you to take your writing out into public, bring the public home to you. Hosting a writing day (or, casting your net more widely, a "creative day") in your home or apartment will ensure you stay on track, and will make the chore of writing more fun. If you do invite friends over, make it clear in your invitation that this will be a work session, and that attendees who don't maintain a minimum level of productivity will be beaten. Include a clear start time and end time in your invitation, and encourage people to be punctual.

Make sure you have enough tables, desks, and chairs set up to accommodate everyone's particular work needs, and make sure that a clock is clearly visible to everyone. Brew up a pot of coffee or tea, and have lots of noncrumbly, nonoily treats on hand so people can snack without worrying about their keyboards.

After everyone's had a chance to settle in, announce a schedule. Thirty or forty minutes of work followed by a ten-minute break is a good one. But it's up to you. Whether you allow talking during the work sessions is also your call, but if you okay conversation during the work period, be sure to have headphones or earplugs on hand so you don't get distracted. Ask all attendees to turn off the ringers on their cell phones, and set a timer so everyone knows exactly when each session ends and the glorious break time begins.

Should anyone continue to type after the alarm marking the end of the session sounds, chop off their fingers. Don't be afraid to be a tyrant.

"Oddly, it only worked for one year," Andrew writes. "Those who get stung by a fanatical NaNoWriMo writer once are going to avoid being stung again in the future."

Some NaNoWriMo winners have upped the ante on their deadlines by putting themselves on payroll. They find a friend willing to play banker and give that person a respectable sum of money. The writer then "earns" a chunk of their money back every week they hit their word-count goals. The catch: Their friend in Accounts Payable gets to keep all money from missed deadlines.

PayPal and other forms of e-banking work better than cash for this because your banker can work in her pajamas, and you get the satisfaction of being paid the same day you submit proof of your

RAISING YOUR OWN NOVELING ARMY

If you're a busy parent, one sneaky way to head off distractions from your kids is by inviting them to write their own books alongside you. NaNoWriMo has a Young Writers Program (ywp.nanowrimo.org) where kids can choose a word-count goal for the month, track their writing progress, exchange encouragement with other budding authors, and download free, fun workbooks that teach fiction-writing basics.

If you decide to give it a shot with your kids, Sonia Rao, a four-time NaNoWriMo winner from Mumbai, India, recommends creating a place in the house where everyone posts their word counts. "Put up a whiteboard with both your names in two columns and with the daily target word count", she says. "Completed, on-target word counts get gold star stickers."

Sonia also found that novel swaps kept things interesting. "Exchange novels every day," she says. "Based on the last few lines, continue the story for 200 or so words. The person whose story it is can discard those words or continue with them. This can be quite an eye- and mind-opening exercise!"

Writing field trips also heighten the excitement around the shared endeavor, says Michael Bergeron, a two-time NaNoWriMo winner from Antelope, California. "Take your son or daughter to a place that is comfortable for both of you to write. Use it as an escape from the normal routine at home."

Tim Yao, a ten-time NaNoWriMo winner from Naperville, Illinois, stresses the importance of making sure the kids stay level-headed even as book fever infects the household. "School comes first," he says. "Be supportive of their NaNoWriMo ambitions but make it very low key and low pressure."

Heather Dudley, a six-time NaNoWriMo winner from Macon, Georgia, agrees. "Emphasize how much fun you have, and how the point is to not worry about sucking. My perfectionist daughter frets over how to spell this, or that, or what comes next. I don't correct her spelling or grammar, but instead rave about the story, and how proud I am that she's completing it."

And if you're lucky enough to have a teen at home, often the best tactic is to just decide on a writing goal together, and then make yourself scarce. "My then-fourteen-year-old daughter won two years ago," says Peg Rousar-Thompson, a five-time NaNoWriMo winner from Racine, Wisconsin. "I'm convinced she stuck with it because I acted completely disinterested in what she was doing."

noveling labors. Another tip: Be sure to find a tough-love money handler who will actually keep the cash if you miss your deadlines. Softies need not apply.

Chore-Based Betting

Those with no savings to put on the line can explore the wonders of chore-based ultimatums. Should you only write 30,000 words next month, for instance, you agree to scrub a friend's kitchen floor. A 20,000-word total means mowing lawns for a month. And should you fail to break 10,000 words, you agree to scoop the poop of your friend's fiercely incontinent dog for an entire year.

You'll find that friends and family warm to this plan immediately. For guaranteed novel-writing results, it's best to construct a web of miserable chore-based bets that would essentially occupy your weekends until you die.

For twelve-time NaNoWriMo winner Dan Strachota of Oakland, California, the conditional betting took place on the home front. "The second year I did NaNoWriMo, my girlfriend and I wrote together at adjacent computers," Dan remembers. "In order to motivate ourselves we would make wagers over who could write the most words in thirty minutes. It would get pretty competitive, as the punishments for losing grew more and more heinous—from easy stuff like having to give back rubs and sing a cappella songs to harder things like running up the street half naked, doing funny dances, and kissing random strangers."

Ah, the timeless power of tender, loving humiliation. Follow Dan's example and get creative in your shackling of yourself to your writing instrument. And remember: A little fear goes a long, long way.

3. NOVELING NESTS, MAGICAL TOOLS, AND A GROWING STOCKPILE OF DELICIOUS INCENTIVES

In her search for a quiet place to write, Karla Akins quickly found that locking herself away in her study brought no relief from the tempests brewing in the house.

"A closed door with children in the house is nothing more than an invitation to bang, kick, scream, and cry," advises Akins, a seven-time NaNoWriMo winner from North Manchester, Indiana. "The teenager will be in an emotional crisis with his girlfriend, and the younger ones are sure you simply cannot survive without being in their presence."

Karla's quest for some writing solace did turn up one unique environment where the children were much less likely to intrude.

"I do a lot of brainstorming and 'writing' on the toilet," she says. "I keep a notebook or small tape recorder with me all the time. It's amazing what kinds of things will come to me while having my 'quiet time.'"

Writers with children can relate to Karla's nomadic quest for quiet. But even if the only other living things you share your home with are houseplants and dust mites, finding a perfect place to write is not easy.

In this chapter, we'll look at the pros and cons of potential noveling environments, from coffee shops to cars to cheap motels. And after we look at where you might write, we'll go shopping for the tools—edible and otherwise—that you'll need to gather for the mammoth literary task ahead.

Writing at Home →

Home is the best option most of us have for pounding out novels. It's familiar, it's open twenty-four hours a day, it's relatively private, and the food and drinks on the menu are as cheap as you'll find anywhere outside of a soup kitchen.

The advantages of home-based working, though, are also its shortcomings. Because your house, apartment, or dorm room is so familiar, you'll likely find it difficult to draw a firm line between "novel time" and "puttering time," "family time," or, most harrowingly, "dish-washing time." A quick trip to the fridge for some glucose reinforcements can turn into an hour-long rearranging of the canned goods in your cupboards. And because you can work as late as you want without employees trying to shoo you out, you're bound to be less focused in your writing, letting noveling take a backseat to other pressing chores that might arise.

All these liabilities can be minimized with a few tips:

1. Isolate yourself as much as possible. ● If you live with other people, try to find a spot where you won't be disturbed. Be creative about it. Try writing in closets, bathrooms, or garages. Anywhere with a door that closes is your friend. If you don't have access to a room with a door, arrange your computer so you're facing a wall, and get some headphones or earplugs. Shut off your phone and, if you can do so without causing an uproar among your family or housemates, disconnect the internet. You can return any calls or emails after your writing session is over.

2. Create uninterrupted blocks of time and limit yourself to them. • Make it clear to yourself and anyone you live with that you will be working, uninterrupted, for a set amount of time—at which point you will stop and rejoin the normal, non-noveling human race. Knowing that you'll be working for a bounded amount of time helps keep you on task, and it will spare any housemates or family members from feeling like they need to tiptoe around you the whole night.

3. Make yourself comfortable. • Find a stable desk or table, and make sure your chair feels good and raises you up to a wrist-friendly typing level.

4. Don't write within view of a bed. • The sweet, sweet temptation of napping is simply too great. If you live in a studio apartment or are otherwise obligated to write in your bedroom, do what I do: Pile a cumbersome assortment of boxes and other heavy items onto your bed to retard the onset of accidental slumbers.

5. Keep your writing area neat. • If you're anything like me, your life is chaotic enough already; give yourself the gift of sitting down to a tidy writing area each day. This doesn't mean, incidentally, that you can't storm and throw things around as you work. I find flinging balls of paper, pens, and other assorted office supplies across the room helps the whole writing process feel more romantically agonized, and I'll throw things for fun even when my novel is going well. But at the close of each session, spend a couple of minutes picking up the papers, coffee mugs, wads of chewing tobacco, and half-eaten animal carcasses and move them all into the kitchen (where they can be more effectively ignored). That way, no matter how messy the rest of your living quarters get, your runway for the next day's literary adventure will be cleared for takeoff.

THE WONDERS OF COFFEE

Ah, sweet caffeine. If you ever needed proof that coffee is the wonder drug for novelists everywhere, you won't after next month. Whether you French-press it, filter-brew it, or buy it in steaming cups from your neighborhood coffee-monger, you will be thankful you have buckets of the bean on hand during your noveling adventure.

Scientists who have studied caffeine's effects on humans have discovered that the drug takes only a few minutes to spread to nearly every cell in the body. It's also a natural antidepressant, elevating moods for up to eight hours per cup. And coffee contains antioxidants whose healthful effects rival those produced naturally by the body.

Coffee's history is a novel in its own right: The drink was first served in Ethiopia, where the leaves, not the beans, were brewed as a tea. Eventually the Yemenis got hold of the magic bean juice, and the coffee craze spread throughout the Arab world and beyond. Sort of. The Yemeni rulers forbade the export of unsterilized beans to the outside world, so supplies remained limited until Dutch traders absconded with a sapling in 1616, raising the purloined plant's offspring in Ceylon. Soon thereafter, the Dutch colonies of Java, Sumatra, and Bali were overflowing with coffee beans, and java junkies the world over breathed a sigh of relief. Over time, the destinies of Haiti, Brazil, and Guatemala have each been radically altered because of their connections to the crop, with the commodity bringing about everything from slave uprisings to political revolutions to utter economic collapse. All part of the rich legacy of the brewed novelist-helper that you're sipping today. Bottoms up!

Creating a Noveling Headquarters Away from Home →

For those who can work in public, the world is a particularly succulent noveling oyster. Laptops, tablets, phones with portable keyboards, and, of course, pen and paper allow writers to take advantage of a host of creativity-spiking writing milieus.

For me, I have to get out of the house to write. Though I live alone, I find the peace and quiet at home insufferably distracting. I also find that my apartment, with its off-the-beaten-path location and cumbersome series of locks, has a real dearth of interesting-looking strangers wandering in off the street looking for coffee.

Working in public gives you that and more. Obsessive email checking is somewhat curtailed, the mood is more lively, and buckets of espresso are there for the taking. Because I have the attention span of an aphid, I tend to seek out new writing environments pretty frequently, particularly ones that are open late. In my search for noveling novelty, I've driven out to the airport to spend the day writing in the concourses, had day-long writing sessions in the local IKEA cafeteria (fantastic views over the San Francisco Bay!), and worked out more than one chapter in the swank, anonymous recesses of downtown hotel bars.

Of all the environments for writing outside the home, though, I've found none more amenable than the café.

Your Novel (Coming Soon to a Café Near You)

The allure of a coffee shop for noveling is obvious: instant access to caffeine, comfortable seats, sturdy tables, and a nonstop stream of potential novel fodder walking by.

These days, the click of computer keys is as ubiquitous as the whirr of the milk steamer. The tech-friendly vibe of most cafés is great news for novel writers, and as you scope out cafés in your area keep an eye out for the following boons:

Plenty of outlets! • If your laptop is as old as mine, the key strategy is jockeying for a good position near the café's electrical outlets. A laptop uses a minuscule amount of power (about a cent per hour)—a cost you can karmically offset by supersizing your drink or getting something to nibble on while you write.

If you feel comfortable doing it, a good way to get around an otherwise great spot's shortage of outlets is to bring a power strip (or three-outlet extender) and an extension cord. I always keep both in my car in November for NaNoWriMo group writing sessions. I also have a roll of electrical tape on hand in case the cord becomes a tripping hazard for other patrons.

Students! • Where there are students, there is a greater-than-average tolerance for "camping," the term staff use to describe people who set up shop at tables for hours at a time. Since your average writing session will probably be about two hours, you'd do well to find a place that won't start giving you the hairy eyeball if you nurse that latte for a while.

Quiet background music! • There's a coffee shop near my house in Berkeley that has it all: convenient location, strong java, comfy seats, and electrical outlets up the wazoo. The café, though, is always on the verge of going out of business. Why? Because the manager has a soft spot for light rock at block-shaking volumes. Hall & Oates are painful at a murmur; turned up loud, they become a health hazard. Don't waste your time trying to write in a place where you can't concentrate.

Starbucks coffee shops are built for abuse by novelists; the music is usually surprisingly good (and inoffensively low) and all of them make a point of making outlets accessible to laptop users. Best of all, as long as you're not setting anything on fire, the staff doesn't care how long you stay.

Expensive Wi-Fi! • The internet eats novels for breakfast. One of the best things a café can do to nurture the literary ambitions of its clientele is to charge through the nose for Wi-Fi.

Sadly, free internet now is the norm in cafés. If you're having trouble unplugging, consider installing one of the many programs that will shut off your internet for a set amount of time.

Libraries

Like coffee shops, libraries have become more hip to the needs of computer users, adding electrical outlets to tables and study carrels. Unlike cafés, libraries will let you stay as long as you like without buying anything. You also have the advantage/distraction of being able to do research as you write.

The library's main drawback is usually an early closing time. If you live close to a university, though, chances are good there will be some college libraries that stay open until 11:00 p.m. or midnight. Call ahead to see if you need a student ID for entry.

Work

As two-time NaNoWriMo winner Irfon-Kim Ahmad can tell you, not all press is good press. When the Torontonian was quoted in a newspaper article about the city's NaNoWriMo participants, his quiet literary project suddenly became a matter of public record at his office. With some surprising results.

"From that point onward," Irfon-Kim says, "everybody at my company would ask me about my word count and how the novel was going every day. I could pretty much work on it openly as long as nothing with a really tight deadline was looming. I think that my boss would have been willing to excuse me from meetings to write if I'd have asked. He was very excited about the whole thing."

While this sounds like a dream setup for most of us, Irfon-Kim soon discovered the complicated nature of bringing personal projects into a working environment.

"It ended up acting as a huge deterrent from writing," Irfon-Kim laments. "Because everybody assumed that I would use company time to write, I went out of my way to prove that I was being productive, and I didn't write at all during working hours. The year before, when I was being furtive about the whole thing, I probably wrote nearly a quarter of my novel at work."

That, in a nutshell, describes the office: It's a wonderful, horrible place to get work done. Its appeal as a novel workshop lies in the lengthy attendance it requires of us each week, and chances are good that while using the Time Finder in Chapter 2 you drooled over all the red-underlined hours you spend at work every day. If you spent just a fraction of your workday typing away at your novel, you'd be able to get the whole book written on company time.

Yet work can be a difficult place to get anything accomplished. The most ethically unencumbered route is to come in to work early or stay late. This also gives you the advantage of writing with fewer distracting coworkers around coming up to ask how your novel is going.

HEARING VOICES: THE POWER OF HEADPHONES

When writing a novel, I *always* wear headphones. Sometimes I even remember to plug them in to something. I love headphones because they help dampen the clatter of the outside world. And when they're hooked into a music player, my rubberized earbuds shove the music directly into my brain in cinematic ways, adding lovely contours to the edges of my thoughts and amplifying sentences as they spray out onto the page.

Headphones, with or without music, also create a social buffer around you. This is especially helpful if you are a woman trying to get your novel written in a café. For a certain type of gregarious person (read: man), the sight of a lady with a furrowed brow typing madly on a laptop in a public place sends the following very clear message: "Please come bother me." Headphones are the perfect foil for keeping these well-meaning, deeply annoying people at bay.

Fellow Toronto resident and one-time NaNoWriMo winner Michele Marques found her company's break room to be a fantastic place to write.

"I think the workplace cafeteria is greatly underrated," Michele reports. "There's good lighting, a flat surface, and a lunch hour. If you bring your lunch, you only have to reheat it and you're ready to write."

And then there's the matter of actually noveling while on the clock. The moral question of stealing company time to work on your novel is a toughie. If you do decide to novel during working hours, there are four practical pointers to keep in mind to make the writing as productive as possible.

1. Tell few (if any) coworkers you're writing the novel until you're finished with it. ● As Irfon-Kim's story proves, once word gets out about your literary feat-in-progress, everyone will start thinking you're working on your novel even when you're doing actual work.

2. Know that, unless you are working with a complete lack of supervision, you can't really relax into your story while you're supposed to be working. ● For this reason, imagination-intensive scenes where you need to improvise clever solutions to vexing plot problems will probably be all but impossible to pull off while you're on the clock. If you know you will write at work, consider tackling the scenes you've already mapped out, so you're simply coloring in the predetermined outlines.

3. Never let your novel touch your work computer's hard drive. ● Keep your work on your own USB thumb drive or save everything directly to the cloud. Keeping the file off your computer desktop makes it less likely a snooping boss will stumble across your masterpiece.

Even saving your work on a portable drive, though, won't completely cover up the tracks of your noveling. The file name and the fact that it originated from an external source will show up in several places on your computer, including the drop-down "recently accessed documents" list on your word processor. Clear your novel file from this list by opening four or five other documents at the end of each day. And you can also make it look less suspicious by naming your novel file something innocuous like "accounts_summary.doc" or "presentation_draft.doc."

4. Be ready to toggle over to a "cover" file at all times. A few well-timed keystrokes can send you smoothly from your personal document into the work-approved sanctuary of an Excel file. Carole McBay, a three-time NaNoWriMo winner from London, recommends the potent alt-tab combination, which immediately toggles you over to another open window. (It's command-tab on a Mac.) If you're going to write at work, practice that keystroke until you can do it with the stealth of a ninja.

Quirky Places

For Carolyn Lawrence, a three-time NaNoWriMo winner from Atlanta, the gym emerged as a surprisingly productive place to get work done.

"Treadmills always get my creative juices flowing," she says, laughing. "Though most of the members of the gym now think that there is something seriously wrong with me, because I talked my plot out loud to myself while working out, all while I was wearing my headphones."

However questionable the results can sometimes be, one of the joys of the noveling journey is applying your creativity to some conventionally uncreative spaces. Necessity is truly the mother of invention, and your tight deadline will transform formerly inert way stations into magical writing hubs. Take advantage of offbeat spaces; they can be a great way to keep your word count high and your imagination stoked.

HOW DO I GET RID OF MY CHILDREN?

For parents, balancing the need for writing time with kids' needs for, well, everything, can add a difficult wrinkle to an already-challenging month. If the notion from Chapter 2 of bringing your kids into the writing fold sounded like too much work, consider these easy tips for balancing parenthood with authorhood.

Kathy Kitts, a ten-time NaNoWriMo winner from Placitas, New Mexico, recommends racking up child-care credits before your noveling month begins. "Trade babysitting with other family and friends in October," she says. "That way, they are already *beholden* to you and can't weasel when November comes around."

Lowering your standards for household cleanliness is also key, says Angela Lindfors, a five-time NaNoWriMo winner from San Antonio, Texas. "Let the house go for a month," she says. "If everyone is fed and no one is sleeping in filth, you're doing fine."

Cylithria Dubois, a thirteen-time NaNoWriMo winner from Kansas City, Missouri, recommends creating some visual aids for your kids, so they can know when you're on duty. "Take a sheet of card stock and fold it in half," she says. "On one side write, 'Mom is in' and on the flip side write 'The Writer is in.' Set this table tent in a visible spot, and flip it according to your writing times."

If your kids are still interrupting you, bribes of shiny objects and extra rations of television always seem to work. "November is the best time to buy them that new video game," says Letitia Jones, a four-time NaNoWriMo winner from High Point, North Carolina. Stefan Ecks, one-time NaNoWriMo winner from Edinburgh, Scotland, swears by the power of online movie marathons. "The *Pingu* episodes pack on YouTube," he says, "has a running time of sixteen hours."

And if your kids are too young to tell time, Rolf Nelson, a four-time NaNoWriMo winner from Providence, Rhode Island, has a tip. "November," he says, "is also National Going-To-Bed-Early Month."

Oakland's Tim Lohnes, the come-from-behind writer from Chapter 2, swears by cheap motel rooms as productive places to get writing done (he uses last-minute deal sites to get hotel rooms in out-of-the-way suburbs).

A more intoxicating option is to write in your neighborhood pub. Four-time NaNoWriMo winner Amy Probst of Detroit, Michigan, likes to drag her writing group to a local watering hole called the Senate.

Amy reports: "My fellow Detroit WriMos and I are fond of putting a mess of quarters in the jukebox down at the Senate for mandatory writing until the music stops. It's good for inspiration. The bar has also provided us with incredible characters and dialogue from the regulars."

I've had similar luck with a brewpub in Oakland. Located next to the Oakland Convention Center, the place is a ghost town after the conventioneers head back to their hotels in the evening. While I was a little nervous to show up at a bar as part of a nerdy writing posse, the staff turned out to be all too glad to have us there.

"It's the laptop people!" one waitress would call excitedly whenever we came in. We *did* get some strange looks from regulars at times, but mostly we were happily left alone to stare intently at our laptop screens while sipping our Guinness.

If you're looking for a *truly* anything-goes bar environment, try a hotel lounge. The stomping grounds of perpetually overworked (and perpetually working) business travelers, hotel bars are laptop-friendly, open late, and offer novelists a front-row seat to the kinds of activities that have filled great novels for centuries: nefarious deals, shady alliances, and steamy, illicit affairs—all accompanied by the salty perk of free cocktail nuts.

The Tools of the Trade →

Like any good vacation, half the fun of writing a novel is getting properly outfitted. A month-long noveling trip requires a shopping spree every bit as enjoyable as a jaunt to the Bahamas. And if you pinch pennies, you can get all the high-tech gear, low-tech tools, and copious amounts of treats you'll need for under $35.

The stuff you need falls neatly into two categories: things you can put in your mouth and things you shouldn't. We'll tackle the inedible writing tools first, and then move on to the essential snacks and drinks.

A Notebook

The universe loves novelists. During the novel-prep and book-writing period, you'll watch, delighted, as the cosmos parts to reveal a rich vein of pilferable, copyright-free material explicitly for your noveling use.

A couple will sit down next to you on the bus and proceed to have an argument that you'll use verbatim as a pivotal turning point in your character's love life. Friends will tell a story about an embarrassing, misrouted email at work, and it will inspire an entire subplot. From random graffiti to raccoon-shaped clouds to heavy-metal ballads on the radio, the natural world will be flinging so many novel-appropriate artifacts, phrases, and characters your way that the most difficult thing during your noveling month will not be finding inspiration but fending off an excess of it.

Your notebook, the most powerful apparatus a novelist can own aside from a coffeemaker, is a bucket for catching the downpour of material the universe provides. Many writers just use the notepad app that comes with their phones, or dictate memos to themselves using the phone's built-in recorder. Both are great, but to me, nothing can beat the romantic appeal of an old-school paper notebook. The notebook you buy should be small enough to fit comfortably into a pocket or purse, and discreet enough for it to be wielded in public without arousing too much suspicion. Avoid spiral-bound notebooks, as they are prone to shedding pages and snagging on clothes.

A Magical Pen

This is the peanut butter to your notebook's jelly, and as with the notebook, it should be somewhere on your person at all times. When picking out your pen, *you must be absolutely sure that you have found the right one.* Don't grab the first ballpoint that catches your eye in the office supply store. The magical pen will be both your conduit of mystery and a documenter of epiphanies. Getting the wrong pen for the job would be a disastrous start to the writing process. Try every pen available, writing phrases like "I am an unstoppable writing dynamo" and "future badass novelist" on the sample pads. After you do this long enough, one pen candidate will rise above the rest. That enchanted implement is the one that has been slated to help you on your noveling journey.

If your workplace happens to have a broad array of pens on hand, you can save money (and a trip to the stationery store) by picking out a winner from the supply cabinet when no one's looking.

A Word-Processing Device

This is the vast digital warehouse for your novel, and it will likely be the one thing on this list of must-haves that you already own. Because of their go-anywhere, can-do attitudes, laptop computers and their tablet cousins are a great tool for the job. If your laptop is somewhat past its prime, you can increase its usefulness by ordering a cheap new battery for it from online auction sites, such as eBay.

Some NaNoWriMo participants swear by an affordable machine called a Neo. This is a battery-powered word-processing device that looks like a cross between a laptop and a children's Speak & Spell. The minuscule screen displays only four lines of text or so at a time, which can be helpful in warding off obsessive editing. The keyboard is large and comfortable, and you can work for up to 700 hours on two AA batteries.

If you're not ready to drop a couple hundred dollars on a new machine, though, don't worry: An old desktop computer, your phone

DEDUCTING YOUR NOVELIST SHOPPING SPREE FROM YOUR TAXES

Want to save a bundle on your noveling notebook, pens, and reference novels? What about a discount on your monthly movie-streaming service? A percentage off your rent or mortgage? Well, read on: As a novelist, you're entitled to deduct all of your novel-writing expenses from your taxes. Maybe.

I talked to Peter Abel, a CPA in Oakland, and asked him to explain the somewhat confusing criteria the IRS uses when deciding what expenses amateur novelists can write off in the pursuit of their muse.

"If you're an artist," Peter says, "there is a great latitude in the things that you do in order to research your craft. The big issue is whether this is a hobby or whether this is a business."

If, like many of us, you are writing your novel just for the fun of it, you are out of luck. But if you do intend to someday make money from your writing, get thee to a CPA right away. Everything that furthers your novel-writing efforts ("research" trips to Hawaii, cable TV, a new computer with a wall-sized screen, etc.) can be deducted from your taxes, as long as you can prove you spent the money in an effort to produce a cash-generating manuscript.

According to Peter, the simplest way to prove your honorable mercantile intentions is to actually sell a book. Since the business of novel writing often consists of years of unprofitable struggle, the IRS allows you to also deduct expenses so long as you document attempts at profitability. These include copies of query letters you send to editors or agents, and logs of phone calls you made hounding your local publisher. Pay for everything you can by credit card so you'll have proof of payment and a receipt. And know that claiming a deduction, especially deducting a home office, does increase your chances of being audited by a percentage point or two.

paired with a wireless keyboard, or even a manual typewriter will do fine. Go with whatever you have access to; NaNoWriMo participants have successfully written 50,000-word novels using everything from voice-recognition software to a magic marker (seriously).

A Reference Book

When you start writing, you'll find grammatical and style questions popping up immediately. Are quotes always set off from descriptive text with indents? How do you handle parenthetical comments that are actually stand-alone sentences? Are you supposed to italicize internal monologues?

A professional editor would tell you to pick up a usage guide like William Strunk Jr. and E. B. White's *The Elements of Style* or, even worse, the *Chicago Manual of Style*. I find both books to be awkwardly laid out and dangerously sleep-inducing. So in the interest of keeping momentum while I write, I keep a copy of Nick Hornby's *High Fidelity* close at hand to use as a template for formatting or style issues. Any book you know and love is a perfect candidate for a reference novel, but this is also a great opportunity to pamper yourself by buying a novel you've been wanting to read for a long time.

Music

Music is the most potent writing drug available without a prescription. Before you start writing, amass as many songs as possible that might be conducive to noveling. Every novel, explicitly or not, has a soundtrack. Finding that soundtrack, and listening to novel- and scene-appropriate music as you write, will help you slip into the sensual realms you're describing. Whether you're tapping into the hyperbolic violence of a horror novel or the prim grace of a historical romance, there's some complementary music out there eager to help you get it written.

I'm a big fan of movie scores, as they tend to be overly dramatic in all the right ways. When your character is striding off for the final showdown with the landlord or the face-eating remora, you don't want to have the Bee Gees cooing about dance fevers in the background. You want the epic rumble of kettle drums and the spiraling scream of an overheated string section. Yaaar!

Whatever your musical predilections, plan on creatin
energy-bolstering mixes for your writing plunge.

A Writing Totem

Spider-Man has his tights; Wonder Woman has those bullet-
deflecting bracelets. Berkeley's Erin Allday has her fingerless
gloves.

"They're a super-cheap pair of black cotton gloves from the
Gap," the twelve-time NaNoWriMo winner explains. "All the fingers are uneven because I'm so bad at using scissors. I pretty much
have to put them on when I get stuck working on my NaNoWriMo
novel. They make me feel so old-school writerly, like I'm some
struggling novelist sitting by candlelight in an apartment that I
can't afford to keep adequately heated. They definitely put me in
the mood to write. It's also a nice tactile distraction, where I'm
focused on my fingers and the actual act of typing instead of staying in my head and trying to make the words sound pretty."

As Erin can attest, you are about to spend a month living far
above the realm of mere mortals, and you, too, need something you
can wear to inspire your superheroic abilities.

A wearable, writing-enhancing object serves several important purposes. First, it helps you transition from the world of everyday living into the fictional realms you've created. In the former
you are a normal person, working a normal job. In the latter, you
are an all-powerful deity capable of laying waste to entire cities
with a few taps of the keyboard.

For me, when I don my plastic Viking helmet, I know I've
left the real world behind and am sailing off to the shores of my
fictional Valhalla. The hat reminds me that I am Elsewhere, and
I will be staying there until the ship's reserves of Dr Pepper and
Starbursts run low.

Putting on a writing cap, cape, wig; or pantsuit will also serve
to remind you that this is a fun, somewhat ridiculous creative

exercise, where the goal is to spend a few weeks writing for the hell of it. For some reason, it's hard to overthink your writing when you're wearing a three-foot-tall Marie Antoinette wig.

Personally, I like to have several tiers of headwear, depending on how my story is coming along. If all's well, I'll wear my baseball hat, the ideal thinking cap for sporty, low-exertion writing. The Viking helmet is for the more complicated passages. And if things are going horribly awry in my novel, I bust out my cowboy hat, which I pull down low over my eyes in a menacing fashion to warn my un-cooperative story that an unholy dose of hurt is about to be unleashed upon it if it doesn't fall into line.

Conveniently, having something special you wear when you write provides a visual cue to anyone you're living with, including small children, that you've slipped away into the shadowy Realm of the Novel, and that you are not to be disturbed unless they—or one of the more likable of the family pets—are on fire.

Eating Your Way to 50,000 Words →

If I had to describe my motivational strategy for drafting a novel in one month, it would be this: treat-o-rama.

Writing a novel is a creative exercise, sure, but it's also a remarkably convenient opportunity to shower yourself with goodies and other pampering items you've gone far too long without having in your life. Allowing yourself loads of restaurant meals, sugary treats, and exotic beverages is the best way to keep your spirits high during the exhausting mental acrobatic routines you'll be pulling off next month as you write.

Takeaway Food from Local Restaurants

Month-long novel writing is like running a marathon: You need to make sure you have the right fuel available at all times, preferably handed to you by strangers as you run past them. Thankfully, there are dozens of restaurants in your area that will serve as your nutritional support staff, all for the price of an inexpensive entree.

Avail yourself of the hospitality of these culinary good samaritans during your noveling month. Remember: You have not been put on this Earth to cook meals for yourself *and* write a novel. Delegate the kitchen work as often as possible, and everyone will be the happier for it.

Mass Meals

If you find the takeout meals are starting to drive you into debt, hit the grocery stores and stock up on the fixin's for Mass Meals. These are the easy-to-prepare-in-vast-quantities entrees that you know and love from institutional cafeterias and buffet lines. Consider an acre-sized pan of lasagna, a two-ton casserole, or a vat of tuna salad. Potatoes can be baked by the dozen, then refrigerated until you're ready to top them with cheese and veggies.

Massive Snacks

Speaking of veggies . . . When you're writing, you'll eat just about anything that lingers near your keyboard for more than thirty seconds, which makes this an excellent time to get caught up on all those boring vitamin- and mineral-laden foods you spend the rest of the year avoiding.

Go crazy in the produce aisle of your favorite grocer and buy a ton of carrots, celery sticks, broccoli, green peppers, and anything else that catches your eye. Then take them home, chop 'em up, and leave them in a bowl of water in the fridge. They'll keep longer that way, and they'll also be crisp and cool when you're ready to graze.

A writer cannot live by celery sticks alone, however. As you wrestle with your novel, you'll need the explosive energy bursts that only a steady diet of manufactured sugar can provide. Stockpile chocolate in all its mouthwatering forms.

The only cautionary question you should ask yourself is, "Can I shove these things into my mouth and then type without leaving residue all over the computer?" Some snacks are more keyboard friendly than others.

Once you've accumulated your weight in junk food, you should dispense it according to the following careful criteria: Did you just finish a paragraph? Have a treat.

Drinks

Beverage scientists have discovered that dehydration is one of the main factors in making a person feel tired. As it's all but impossible to work on your novel while you're collapsed over your keyboard asleep, you should constantly pump your body full of fluids while working.

Water, however boring, is a must. But having lots of adventuresome drinks on hand also makes the novel-writing process a little more exciting, with each trip to the refrigerator mirroring your own literary voyage of discovery. So go wild at the grocery store when you stock up, getting both old favorites and some new oddities. Mango-choco-guava nectar? Sure! Pomegranate-beet soda? You bet!

And don't forget to load up on the warm drinks as well. Coffee, tea, and hot chocolate are soothing balms for frazzled synapses. In addition to serving as excellent caffeine conduits, their warmth is physically reassuring, and their slow-sipping properties make them the perfect noveling pause. It also feels wonderfully picturesque and romantic to have a steaming beverage near your computer while you're working, especially if someone is going to be dropping by to see how the writing is going.

4. CRUISING FOR CHARACTERS, PANNING FOR PLOTS, AND THE FIRST EXCITING GLIMPSES OF THE BOOK WITHIN

After months of preparation, Jennifer McCreedy had an absolutely clear vision of how her intricate fantasy novel would unfurl.

"I churned out character biographies, world maps, and language keys," says the one-time NaNoWriMo winner from Detroit. "I had developing cultures, societies, religions, hierarchical class structures—even regional clothing, genetic quirks, weapons, and customs."

When the month began, Jennifer dove in with all of her notes at her side—and promptly stopped writing.

"I did so much developmental work on the novel that when it came time to actually write it, I was horrified at what I was coming up with. I'd committed too much to making a complete world for my novel just to watch it crumble under the needs of a November 30th deadline. So I set it aside for future work and started completely anew."

Jennifer's experience echoes the dismay of thousands of National Novel Writing Month participants who have brought months or years of novel ideas to the writing table and ended up finding them to be more of a hindrance than a help in getting something written.

It may be counterintuitive, but when it comes to novel writing, more preparation does not necessarily produce a better book. In fact, too much preparation has a way of stopping novel writing altogether. As reassuring as it is to embark on your writing journey with a mule-team's worth of character traits, backstories, plot twists, metaphors, and motifs, it's also a 100 percent viable strategy to walk into the wilds of your novel with nothing but a bottle of water and a change of underwear.

That said, some amount of planning and predeparture decision making can be incredibly helpful. And few things in life rival the fun of sitting in a coffee shop with your notebook and pen contemplating the delicious inventory of ideas, people, places, and expressions that might work well in your book. Even if you're going to improvise your plot as you write, it will help in the long run if you ruminate a little on what kinds of things you'd like to write about.

The planners out there should feel free to completely bury their homes and apartments in plot notes, character lists, story outlines, city maps, costume drawings, evocative photos, and encouraging quotes. If you're looking for an in-depth planning helper, you might want to check out *Ready, Set, Novel!*, a workbook I coauthored with NaNoWriMo's Lindsey Grant and Tavia Stewart-Streit. We packed it with fun activities, prompts, and coloring opportunities (yep) that will open up every nook and cranny of your novel.

So plan to your heart's content! With one catch: You only get one month, maximum, to research and outline before you start writing.

The Happy Side Effects of
Limited Planning →

I know one month seems like a very short amount of time for laying out an entire novel but, trust me: It's perfect. Thirty days or so gives you enough time to get some good ideas on paper, but it prevents the deadly onset of overplanning, which is dangerous for three reasons:

1. If you give yourself too much time to plan, you might end up stumbling across a brilliant concept for your novel. ✎ The last thing you want heading into your noveling month is a brilliant concept. Every year during National Novel Writing Month, I get emails from people jubilantly informing me that they're dropping out of the contest because they've found a story they love and they want to work on it slowly enough to do it justice.

When I check in with these people six months later, they've inevitably stopped working on the book entirely. Why? Because they've become afraid of ruining their book by actually sitting down and writing it.

A novel rough draft is like bread dough; you need to beat the crap out of it to make it rise. Once you stumble across a fantastic, once-in-a-lifetime idea for a book, it's hard to treat that story with the irreverent disregard needed to transform it from a great idea into a workable rough draft. When give yourself just one month to flesh out your concept, you won't have time to feel overly protective of your ideas. And you will therefore stand a much better chance of bringing them to life.

2. Past a certain point, novel planning just becomes another excuse to put off novel writing. ✎ You will never feel sufficiently ready to jump into your novel, and the more time you spend planning and researching, the more likely you'll feel pressure to pull off a masterwork that justifies all your pre-writing work. Give yourself the gift of a pressure-free novel, and just dive in.

3. Prewriting, especially if you're very good at it, bleeds some of the fun out of the noveling process. ✦ Nothing is more boring than spending an entire month simply inking over a drawing you penciled out months earlier. With a tight planning timeline, you'll still have lots of questions about your book when you start writing. Which is great. It makes the writing process one of happy discoveries and keeps the levels of surprise and delight high for you as an author.

So as you look over the gaggle of questions about character, plot, setting, and language in the rest of this chapter, know that they are by no means meant as a rigorous checklist to be completed before starting your novel. They're just a way to help you figure out what you love in novels and, by extension, what you might like to put in yours.

The Two Magna Cartas →

Let's start our discussion of your book with a quick exercise.

Using your noveling notebook and pen of wonder, jot down answers to the following question: What, to you, makes a good novel?

It's an excruciatingly broad question, but give it a shot. And feel free to be as vague or as nerdily detailed as you like; this list can include anything from ultrashort chapters to ribald sex scenes to massive infusions of ill-tempered elves. Anything that floats your fictional boat should go on the list.

My list, to help give you some ideas, looks like this:

    first-person narration

      quirky characters

- ☑ true love
- ☑ found objects
- ☑ disappointment
- ☑ music
- ☑ catharsis
- ☑ feisty old people
- ☑ strong, charismatic protagonists
- ☑ improbable romances
- ☑ smart but unpretentious writing
- ☑ urban settings
- ☑ cliffhanger chapter endings
- ☑ characters who are at turning points in their lives
- ☑ books set in the workplace
- ☑ happy endings

Okay, now make your list. Go crazy, and take as long as you want.

Once you've finished, frame it. This document will be your Magna Carta for the next month, helping you channel your awesome writing powers for the good of the people.

Why is this list so frame-worthy?

Because the things that you appreciate as a reader are also the things you'll likely excel at as a writer. These bits of language, color, and technique, for whatever reason, make sense to your creative brain. These are the Things You Understand. And, as you draw the basic outlines of your novel over the next week, you should try to fill that outline in with as many of the juicy elements from the Magna Carta as possible.

If you like it when authors start chapters with quotations, for instance, start gathering some pithy zingers for your story. Are coming-of-age tales your guilty pleasure? Consider setting your story at a summer camp. The chances are good that if a mood, motif, or plot device resonates with you as a reader, you'll be able to adeptly wield it when you're in the writer's seat as well.

Okay, that's the first list. Now on to its equally important sibling...

For the second list, write down those things that bore or depress you in novels. Again, feel free to be as specific or wide-ranging as you like. And be honest. If you don't like books where the words-to-pictures ratio favors the text too heavily, write that down. We're not here to judge. We just want to understand you better.

My list would include the following:

- ☑ irredeemably malicious main characters
- ☑ books set on farms
- ☑ mentally ill main characters
- ☑ food or eating as a central theme
- ☑ ghosts
- ☑ dysfunctional sibling dramas
- ☑ books consisting largely of a character's thoughts
- ☑ weighty moral themes
- ☑ books set in the nineteenth century
- ☑ unhappy endings

Now it's your turn. Write down anything and everything that bores you or brings you down in a book. Go.

When you're finished, frame this list as well. We'll call it Magna Carta II, the Evil Twin of Magna Carta I.

As you spend the next week thinking about what you want to have in your novel, keep MCII close at hand, so you'll remind yourself what *not* to put in your story.

I know it seems silly to have to remind yourself to keep things you dislike out of your novel, but be warned: The stealthy entries on your MCII list are vicious, cunning little buggers, and given the slightest opening, they *will* find their way into your book.

The reason they'll make their way onto your pages is related to the same scientific principle of self-betterment that causes us to bring highbrow tomes home from the bookstore knowing full well they'll go straight onto the bookshelf and never be touched again until our kids move us and our possessions into that miserable senior home down the road.

We buy these difficult books because we feel that, while not very exciting, they are in some way *good* for us. It's a sort of literature-as-bran-flake philosophy: If something is dry and unpalatable, it must be doing something good to our constitutions. This kind of thinking also carries over to the writing realm. If we're worried that our story is lacking in substance, the first thing most of us automatically reach for to fix it are the bran morsels from the MCII.

Still not convinced? Let me offer a real-world example.

When sitting down to craft my second month-long novel, I decided that my previous work—a story about an American music nerd secretly in love with his Scottish green-card wife—had been high on fluff and low on substance.

I was right. So, on my second work, I committed myself to writing a Serious Book. Lacking any appropriately substantial ideas, I simply saddled an otherwise enjoyable main character with an ever-lengthening roster of mental illnesses, suicidal relatives, and ghosts, handily crushing the protagonist's spirit under the pressure of weighty moral themes.

In my quest for writing that would last for generations, I managed to write a book that wore out its welcome in less than three days. Having packed almost every single item on my MCII list into one overwrought package, I lost interest in the main character and her morose life after about 5,000 words, and it was just out of sheer stubbornness, force of will, and a terrifying dearth of any other plausible novel ideas that I was able to see the book through to its predictably depressing finale.

The lesson here is this: If you won't enjoy reading it, you won't enjoy writing it. If you truly are fascinated by the plight of the nation's mentally ill, the ongoing politicization of religious sects in Saudi Arabia, or inner city high-rise housing projects as metaphors for racial injustice and miscarried modernization, by all means put them in your book.

But if, in your heart of hearts, you really want to write a book about a pair of superpowered, kung-fu koalas who wear pink capes and race through the city streets on miniature go-karts, know that this is also a wonderful and completely valid subject for a novel.

As you plan your book this week, remember, above all else, that your novel is not a self-improvement campaign. Your novel is a jubilant hoedown set to your favorite music, a thirty-day visit to a candy store where everything is free and nothing is fattening. When thinking about possible inclusions for your novel, always grab the guilty pleasures over the bran flakes. Write your joy, and good things will follow.

Your Book in Ten Questions or Less →

The gilded MCI and dreaded MCII have provided you with a personalized list of noveling dos and don'ts. Now it's time to put these insights to use in thinking about your story and its characters, plot, setting, and point of view.

Shady Characters

Whether you noticed or not, from the minute you decided to write a novel in a month, the Central Casting wing of your imagination began contemplating contenders for the dramatis personae. Over the next week, you'll start seeing friends and strangers in a different, more apprising light. From the muttering, pimply florist who sells tulips in front of the grocery store to the executive who talks in hushed tones about her evening's sexual conquests on the subway ride to work, the personality traits, quirks, and annoyances of those around you will suddenly be transformed into rich potential fodder for your novel.

But with the huge number of possible characters vying for a role in your book, how do you know who should get the part?

Your Magna Carta I is a great place to start. Looking over my list, I would be wise to keep my eyes peeled for a main character who lives in an urban setting, has a quirky job (maybe working with feisty old people?), and tends to be hopelessly entangled in a quest for true love. (In fact, this describes the main characters in half the books I've written.)

RESEARCH MADE PAINLESS: THE FIVE-CLICK GOOGLE

In doing research for your book, it's easy to get overwhelmed by the enormous number of things you don't know about your subject. To make sure I don't end up in a whimpering, panicked ball underneath my computer, I've come up with a novel-research technique I call the Five-Click Google. Say, for instance, I want to set my upcoming novel in Singapore, and base it on the life of the bartender who invented the Singapore Sling cocktail. I'm not sure why this seems like a good idea, but my heart's set on it.

Do I know anything about Singapore? No. Have I ever consumed a Singapore Sling? Nope.

Great. This is where the Five-Click Google comes in. I bring up Google and type "Singapore Sling," "history," and "Singapore" and hit enter. Now the entirety of my research is to be accomplished in five of the 1,040,000 hits Google has found that match my query.

Thanks to the all-knowing nature of the internet, those five clicks are actually surprisingly bountiful. In less than twenty minutes, I know that the drink was invented in the 1920s by a bartender named Ngiam Ton Boon at the Raffles Hotel in Singapore, and that the drink is a cherry brandy cocktail that sells for an extortionate $21. I also learn that the Raffles Hotel was a hot spot for writers in the first few decades of the twentieth century, and that W. Somerset Maugham haunted the grounds for years, penning odes to the Orient.

A famous writer. An infamous drink. And a coming war that would change their destinies forever. I can hear the voice-over for the movie version of my book already. Thanks, Google!

But another great rule for choosing good characters is to simply pick people you would enjoy getting to know better. Remember: You will be spending *a lot* of time with these people. As you consider a possible character for your story, ask yourself this question: How would you feel about going on a month-long cruise with them? Even the unsavory characters in your book—the black-hearted villains and nine-headed gorgons—should be interesting enough that you wouldn't mind playing shuffleboard or sharing the lobster buffet with them every day for a month.

And once you've decided you're going to invite someone onboard your noveling vacation, sit them down with a Mai Tai on the poop deck and ask them as many questions as you can cram into your seven allotted research days. Some good questions include the following:

How old are they? • In some ways, a character's age will decide the timbre of your story, and each age comes with its own set of desires, dreams, challenges, and financial realities. The "write what you know" contingent would probably advise that you only have characters your age or younger. I'm in the "write what you'd like to know more about" camp, so I say the life cycle's the limit. It's true, however, that it will be easier for you to write characters who are close to your current age.

What is their gender? • Writing across gender lines (meaning male authors have female lead characters, and vice versa) is a snap for some people and completely untenable for others. If you're not sure what sex you want your main character/s to be, I'd recommend writing your novel from your own sex's standpoint. This is especially true if this is your first novel.

Once you decide on their sex, begin thinking of ways you can plumb it for plot wrinkles or juicy potential conflicts. If your character is female, where does she depart from traditional notions of femininity? If your character is a man, is he stereotypically male? Or does he cry at commercials featuring babies and kittens?

What do they do for work? • If your character is between the ages of twenty-one and sixty-five, he or she is likely going to spend a vast portion of the novel at work. Whether you depict your characters' time on the clock is up to you. As I mentioned in my Magna Carta list, I *love* to fill my novels with the weird goings-on at offices and workplaces. Jobs are places where people who have no business ever meeting spend more time together than most married couples, making work an ideal hotbed for plot-generating alliances, rivalries, and schemes.

Who are their friends, family, and love interests? • The more close friends and nearby family a character has, the more material you'll have for your book. But a larger social circle also means more work for you as a writer (this is especially true if your character has children living at home). Because I am a lazy novelist who gets overwhelmed when I have to juggle more than a couple of characters, I am a sucker for protagonists who have just ended a relationship (instant emotional resonance!) and who have recently moved to a new place (blank social slate!).

More imaginative writers can be a little more ambitious in their cast, but my one big piece of advice for first-time authors is this: Keep it simple. Fifty thousand words will come *much* faster than you think; getting bogged down in a long digression about the protagonist's second-cousins will give you less time to focus on the meat of your book.

What is their living space like? • This question isn't about general location, which we'll discuss under "setting," but about the inside of a character's apartment, kitchen, or bedroom. The way people organize their home often mirrors the way they organize their life, and descriptions of the microcosm of the home front are often nicely subtle ways to flesh out each character's likes, dislikes, and neuroses.

What are their hobbies? • I love afflicting my characters with a wealth of strange pastimes, from arcane collecting manias to participation in obsolete and pathetic sports. What do your characters do when they're not at work? And who do they meet while doing it? Are they on a team? Do they take classes? What attracts them to the hobbies they do have, and how much time do they give over to recreational pursuits?

What were they doing a year ago? Five years ago? • This is where we get into the nebulous world of "backstory"—the things that happened to the characters before the book began. Some characters are entirely consumed by something—a murder, a breakup, a misplaced winning lottery ticket—that continues to haunt the rest of their lives. You may or may not choose to allude to these things in the book, but knowing what a few of them are will help give you a deeper understanding of your character.

Because I have trouble enough coming up with a front story before I write, I usually let various backstories emerge during the writing process. If you already have some pretty well-defined characters, you could start delving into backstory now: What did they think they were going to be when they grew up? Did they miss their high school prom? Who in their life has had the biggest influence on them? How has their life turned out differently than they had expected?

What are their values and politics? • Your characters' ideologies and politics will probably rarely come up directly in the novel, but slipping some telling reactions into the book's background can help flesh out each character's personality. Questions you can ask might include: How would your characters respond to being asked for change by a homeless person? When was the last time they went to church? How do they feel about violent media?

Hatching Your Plot

This is the biggie. If there's one thing that keeps most people from diving into novel writing, it's an absence of the mysterious thing called plot.

As intimidating as it seems, plot is simply the movement of your characters through time and over the course of your book. Which means that by having characters in your book, you're guaranteed to have a plot. The plot may be subtle, or it may be the kind of thing that causes people to walk into trees because they couldn't put your book down. It's up to you.

Some writers are dazzlingly adept at coming up with the series of unexpected developments and juicy revelations that we commonly regard as a story's plot. If you are one of these people, you are lucky indeed, and the chances are good that you already have a semicomplete story arc in mind for next month's project.

If you do already have a sense of your plot, I recommend you spend as much time as possible "pitching" it to yourself before writing. Talk through the story from start to finish, as if you were laying it out for a particularly patient agent or producer. Be sure to explain the climaxes and the highlights, and try to add a couple of minutes onto your pitch with each retelling.

For the rest of us, the great majority who are unsure of what exactly will, or should, be happening to our characters next month, I say this: Fear not. No plot truly is no problem. The act of writing is a 100 percent reliable plot-forge. It may seem a little scary to leave your story's backbone to chance, but fusing character and setting into an engaging, readable narrative is what our imaginations are best at. Just focus on creating vivid, enjoyable characters, and a plot will unfold naturally from their actions. As I discovered the first time out, characters will eventually *demand* that certain actions be taken, and there's something uniquely thrilling in that moment when you see them take charge.

However, you *can* help the plot percolation process along by taking another gander at your Magna Carta I list. Which of the story-oriented items from that list seem most exciting to you as a writer? And which of the things you love would lend themselves well to a short-term novel-writing feast?

Also, if you already have an idea of your characters, you can help sketch out the first plot points by taking some time to think about the dramatic changes, turning points, or horrible events you could inflict on them over the course of the book.

Here are some time-tested plot providers to consider: Can someone in your story get fired? Can a marriage or relationship implode? Can someone get a disease? Can someone die? Can an unexpected windfall occur? Can someone be wronged, and set out to exact vengeance? Can someone find a precious or unusual object? Can your character set off on an impossible quest or journey? Can someone try to become something they're not? Can someone fall in love with someone who is off-limits or wildly inappropriate? Can your character be mistaken for someone else?

If all of these questions sound suspiciously familiar, it's because one of them (coupled with the all-important "What would happen if we added an orangutan to the mix?") has driven the plot of nearly every movie you've ever watched and every book you've ever read.

Some might bemoan the fact that the world's plots can be distilled into a quarter page's worth of clichés, but I see it as just further proof of the miraculous power of well-told stories. No matter how many times we hear tales of a pluckish underdog triumphing over an all-powerful foe, we still respond to it. Ditto for romantic comedies. Even when the endings are obvious, we usually don't care so long as the story is well told, with protagonists we can love and antagonists we can throw things at—and with the details grounded in the particulars of their lives and situations.

Which is yet another reason why you shouldn't beat yourself up trying to develop an exciting or original plot right now. A good plot is less a matter of innovation and invention as it is one of creative reuse; the most acclaimed books of the modern era have used the same building blocks as the worst soap operas and clumsiest cartoons. The main thing separating the mind-blowing, life-changing stories of a great novel from the treacly dreck of daytime TV is the manner in which the tale is told. And this telling is the very thing that will emerge out of the clang and sweat of your weekly blacksmithing next month.

Besides, just because a plot idea heading into your novel feels hackneyed doesn't mean the resulting book will be. As you write your rough draft, the story will take itself in directions you'd never intended. What starts out as a word-for-word rewrite of *Jurassic Park* may end up as a historical dramedy set in a Portuguese barber's underpants. It's just the way writing works. Just when you think you know where it's going, it zooms off in a new, unpredicted direction. Don't get me wrong: The quest for originality is an admirable one, and it's something you should definitely think about when you rewrite your manuscript. For now, though, grab whatever tropes or clichés appeal to you and *go*. You'll be surprised at the quirky plot twists and inspired characters you come up with when you stop worrying so much about being innovative.

Background on Backdrops

Happily, most novel ideas suggest their own settings. A story about rampaging zombies terrorizing a Coldplay concert, for instance, would best be set in a medium-sized town—the cemetery in a small town probably wouldn't be able to produce enough zombies, and a big city would have too sizable a zombie-repelling security force. Or if you're writing a quirky romance about two people who meet on an online dating service for agoraphobics, most of your story will occur inside apartments, with an occasional minuscule restaurant or airless bar thrown in for nights on the town.

In my experience, the trick of drafting a setting for your novel is in *modeling*. The more you can base the cemeteries, amphitheaters, and claustrophobic restaurants on real-life versions of those things, the more mental energy you'll have for the truly important aspects of writing—eating the chocolate reserves you've stockpiled, bragging about your progress to attractive strangers at parties, and demanding wrist massages from loved ones.

If possible, set your story in the area where you currently reside. If setting the book on familiar turf is not an option, consider having your story take place somewhere you've always wanted to go. This will make writing your novel a little like a vacation, but without all the ragged hours spent stuck in airports. And if you're planning on inventing an entirely new fantasy world for your characters to frolic in, consider drawing out a basic map of the area before you start the actual writing. Improperly routing your orcs to the

NEW BOOKS, OLD BOOKS, AND THE HIGH COST OF MONKEYS

One of National Novel Writing Month's rules is that you must start your novel from scratch on Day One of the event. You can bring as many outlines and notes and character maps as you like, but writing any of the book's actual prose in advance is forbidden. This rule is enforced by legions of invisible guilt-monkeys, which are unleashed every year against those who break the rules.

While this costs NaNoWriMo a pretty penny in guilt-monkeys, it also keeps things fresh and prevents people from sabotaging their productivity by being overly invested in the outcome of their book.

That said, a growing number of NaNoWriMo veterans have been using the month to add 50,000 more words to an existing manuscript. We call them Rebels, and their ranks include many of our published participants.

If you are going to use your thirty-day deadline to flesh out an existing manuscript, know that a state of exuberant imperfection is harder to attain when you're building a new wing onto an old house. The writing will be slower and the joyful epiphanies fewer. If this is your first month of literary abandon, I strongly recommend you dive in with a new idea.

If you're set on adding 50,000 words to an older story next month, though, here are some great tips from experienced Rebels on doing it with aplomb.

"Spend October (or whatever month comes before your chosen one) getting reacquainted with your novel. Try to think of it as a favourite TV series with a new season about to start. Build up some anticipation! When you begin writing, start a new text document, and use the old one only for reference. It will make getting an accurate word count easier, and will keep you from editing when you should be writing."

—PAZ ALONSO, EIGHT-TIME NANOWRIMO WINNER FROM FRANKFURT AM MAIN, GERMANY

"Whatever you write will probably seem to pale in comparison to what you've spent hours or years writing. What works for me is to embrace the fact that what I add is probably going to seem terrible at first, and plan on rewriting."

—CANDICE ROBINSON, SEVEN-TIME NANOWRIMO WINNER FROM CALGARY, CANADA

"Find a place in the existing plotline where you can add a significant detour, instead of trying to shoehorn in lots of small segments."

—MARA JOHNSTONE, TEN-TIME NANOWRIMO WINNER FROM SANTA ROSA, CALIFORNIA

"Keep a timeline of events, both about what you've written and what you're going to write."

—MANDI LYNCH, SEVEN-TIME NANOWRIMO WINNER FROM NASHVILLE, TENNESSEE

"Don't worry about making sure the new writing matches the tone of the previous chapters. It all has to be edited eventually, and right now the important thing is just getting through the scenes."

—NICOLE TUBERTY, SIX-TIME NANOWRIMO WINNER FROM ST. LOUIS, MISSOURI

swampy Scarr of Bectkdor when they should be advancing on the foreboding Mountains of Mignal can cause no end of headaches in the re-write period.

Wherever you end up setting your story, don't worry too much about lending an enormous amount of realistic detail to the tale's backdrop. In the same way that a theater set will use two or three potted trees to suggest a forest, so should you leave much of your setting to the reader's imagination in the first draft. The editing stage will be the time to painstakingly fill in all of the parks, bars, and stores that make up your fictional world. With writing time in short supply, it's important to scrimp on the small stuff so you can get the overall gist of the story down before crossing the finish line.

When your story takes place will also have a pretty profound effect on the amount of carpentry work required when preparing your novel's sets. Setting your book in the past or future will require more mental energy than ones where you can borrow the cultural mores, architecture, and technological topography of the present.

If you do decide to set your book in the past or future, be sure to use the same half-assed approach to getting the details right as you would with any aspect of the setting. Having the historically appropriate wool weave on your nineteenth-century character's knee socks, or detailing the quantum physics powering your twenty-third-century Starhopper should always take a backseat to getting the basics of your story written.

FAQs on POVs

Though it's the last thing we discuss in this chapter, point of view is the first writerly decision revealed to readers. As you think about your characters, you also need to think about the perspective you'll be using to detail their exploits. You essentially have two choices: first person or third person.

Most of you probably remember discussions of first and third person from seventh-grade English classes. In case you're a little rusty, the best way to understand the difference is to think of your story as a movie. In first-person stories, the movie is shot through a single camera glued to the space between your main character's eyebrows. In third person, you get to use as many cameras as you like, and you can place them anywhere, from the bottom of a blimp passing over the city to an ant hiking up your character's shoe.

The first-person perspective is immediately comfortable for first-time novelists because it echoes the language we use when telling stories in conversations, emails, letters, and journal entries. It's also very conducive to high-speed noveling, since you can spend as much time as you like paddling around in the bottomless depths of a character's thoughts.

If you are writing in an "I"-based narration style, though, know that you will be trapped in one body for the whole story unless you add additional narrators. Ultimately, what this means is that if your main character wants to leave a party just as you're starting to enjoy yourself, you have to go home as well. When your character wants to take a nap, the story stops. And if something essential happens while they're in the bathroom, you'll miss it.

Going with third person, on the other hand, lets you see all of the action, regardless of how long your characters spend in the bathroom. In third-person point of view, the characters, all of whom are described as "he" or "she," are more or less interchangeable from a narrative perspective.

Third person gives you the power of monitoring the words, actions, and thoughts of everyone in a scene. With the third-person, the field of view is reduced, but that limitation means less running around for you as the writer.

Ultimately both POVs are great, and you'll just need to decide which works best with the tone of your story. And you don't need to commit to just one: Feel free to play around with first and third person as you go, letting different characters tell their sides of the story. Sometimes passing the narration hat can save both story and author when things in the book hit a difficult point.

TIPS FROM THE TRENCHES:
NANOWRIMO WINNERS ON PLANNING

"If you, like me, aren't a very visual thinker and can't be bothered with inventing your characters' appearances from scratch, 'cast' real life actors for their roles."
—BEN BYRIEL, ONE-TIME NANOWRIMO WINNER FROM VEJLE, DENMARK

"A quick search for 'random (item/name/description/location) generator' can work wonders. I once had a character whose favourite sandwich was peanut butter and cucumber, thanks to a random sandwich generator. That gave me loads to play with throughout the rest of the novel!"
—CARMEN FOWLE, SEVEN-TIME NANOWRIMO WINNER FROM PORT MOODY, CANADA

"I base a lot of my character's personality and history off of their name. Looking at names with special meanings on baby-naming websites ends up inspiring a lot about my stories."
—CYRENE KREY, ONE-TIME NANOWRIMO WINNER FROM ROSCOE, ILLINOIS

"There are two things I pay attention to when meeting a person for the very first time: their eyebrows and their shoes. Both can give you a lot of insight into a person, so when I'm fleshing out a character, I start there and then expand to their wardrobe as a whole."
—ELIZABETH GREGG, THREE-TIME NANOWRIMO WINNER FROM OAKLAND, CALIFORNIA

"Use your own irritating habits to inform the habits of your characters."
—JANE ORMOND, THREE-TIME NANOWRIMO WINNER FROM MELBOURNE, AUSTRALIA

"Sometimes, if I can't tell if the name works for a character, I try yelling it out loud. You know, as if they're falling off a cliff and I've got to catch them. If it sounds right, it's a keeper."
—SARA HARRICHARAN, SEVEN-TIME NANOWRIMO WINNER FROM PARROTTSVILLE, TENNESSEE

"If you think about your novel as you go to sleep, chances are you'll have thought (or dreamt!) an idea. Keep a notepad and pen by your bed."
—KATHERINE STUBBS, EIGHT-TIME NANOWRIMO WINNER FROM DARWIN, NORTHERN TERRITORY, AUSTRALIA

"For my first month-long novel, I made a mix before I started. Eighteen songs, eighteen chapters. Each chapter had to include something from the song that matched it."
—**JANE RAWSON,** THREE-TIME NANOWRIMO WINNER FROM FOOTSCRAY, AUSTRALIA

"Buy extra underwear for your entire family in October."
—**KATHY KITTS,** TEN-TIME NANOWRIMO WINNER FROM PLACITAS, NEW MEXICO

"Use your phone as a notepad. Once I was at the totally insane Consumer Electronics Show in Las Vegas and passed a booth selling autographed pictures of the cast of *Star Trek: The Next Generation*. I wondered about the company that collected those autographs, and wrote that down on my phone. I used it in the book, along with about 20 other different notions that came to me when I was not in a position to write. People like to ask writers where they get their ideas. I know where I get mine: From my iPhone!"
—**JASON SNELL,** SIX-TIME NANOWRIMO WINNER FROM MILL VALLEY, CALIFORNIA

"TVTropes.org is a massive help. Just don't get sucked in!"
—**DANNI LAWRENCE,** THREE-TIME NANOWRIMO WINNER FROM SOUTHAMPTON, UNITED KINGDOM

"Google Maps is my best friend. You can move through the inside of the Palace of Versailles, or study the fallout zone of the Chernobyl explosion. Exquisitely simple and endlessly helpful!"
—**LUCY RALSTON,** FOUR-TIME NANOWRIMO WINNER FROM ATHENS, GEORGIA

"Real estate websites. They are wonderful for finding great houses you would otherwise never be able to enter, finding inspiration for crazy cellars, wacky art, and amazingly weird furniture."
—**MARRIJE SCHAAKE,** NINE-TIME NANOWRIMO WINNER FROM UTRECHT, THE NETHERLANDS

"Figure out what your character eats for breakfast. Do they like fair trade berries in organic yogurt, or sugary cereal in the shape of cartoon characters? If you're writing historical fiction, fantasy, or sci-fi, the mundane details can become roadblocks if you have to figure them out on the fly. This way you're ready."
—**SOPHIA VOLPI,** FIVE-TIME NANOWRIMO WINNER FROM CHARLOTTESVILLE, VIRGINIA

SECTION *

WRITE HERE!
WRITE NOW!

A Frantic, Fantastic Week-by-Week
Overview to Bashing Out Your Book

* For maximum effect, read each of the following four chapters at
the beginning of their corresponding weeks. **No skipping ahead!**
Peeking at Week Two's pep talk while you're still exploring the
exciting terrain of Week One will cause strange and disquieting
rifts in the temporal fabric of the universe, and may needlessly
jeopardize the lives of everyone on this planet. Be a responsible
global citizen and take the chapters one week at a time.

5. WEEK ONE: TRUMPETS BLARING, ANGELS SINGING, AND TRIUMPH ON THE WIND

Dear Writer,

Here it is: Day One. We're standing together on the precipice that overlooks the vast, uncharted territory of your novel. It's quite a view.

Every author you've ever admired started out at this same point, gazed out with the same mix of wonder and trepidation at that small, verdant speck on the horizon called The End. You are ready, poised. The sun is shining, the birds are singing, and there's an unmistakable smell of victory in the air.

There's also an unmistakable smell of hot dogs wafting over from the Noveling Viewing Platform Snack Shop in the main parking lot.

Mmmm . . . victory and hot dogs. Does life get any sweeter?

It just might.

For, in a matter of minutes, you'll be setting out on your great noveling adventure. As unbelievable as it may seem, in just one month's time you will have written a book the size of the one you are now holding. On the path to noveldom, you'll ford rushing rivers of adversity, and repel countless attacks by television shows, status updates, and other bewitching distractions as you hack tirelessly through brambly questions of character, plot, and setting.

At the end of it all, you'll stand on that faraway, majestic peak, your sore arms raised in a gesture of total literary triumph.

The lessons you take from your travels across Novel-land this month will serve you well throughout the rest of your life. You will walk away from the four-week escapade with a mischievous sense of boldness and an increased confidence in your creative abilities. You will read differently, and write differently, and for better or worse, you will begin seeing the world with the ever-hungry eyes of a novelist.

And before you set off on your valiant and overcaffeinated mission, there's one thing I'll need to take from you.

I'll need to confiscate your Inner Editor.

That's right, the Inner Editor. The doubting, self-critical voice that we all inherited around puberty as an unfortunate door prize for surviving childhood. The Inner Editor is a busybody and perfectionist, happiest when it's tsk-tsking our shortcomings and weaving our past blunders into a rich tapestry of personal failure.

For reasons not entirely clear to anyone, we invite this fun-spoiling tyrant along with us on all our artistic endeavors. And from painting to music-making to writing, our endeavors have paid the price of this killjoy's presence. Thanks to the Inner Editor's merciless second-guessing, most of our artistic output ends up tentative and truncated, doomed to be abandoned at the first sign that the results are anything short of brilliant.

The fear of doing things imperfectly turns what should be fun, creative endeavors into worrisome tasks. With the Inner Editor on board, completing any extracurricular activity you haven't already mastered is like trying to ride a bicycle uphill while towing a rhinoceros in a wagon behind you.

This month, we lose the rhino.

Because this month, you'll leave your Inner Editor here with me at the fully licensed, board-certified *No Plot? No Problem!* Inner Editor Kennel—where it can spend its days carping with other Inner Editors, happily pointing out typos on blogs and complaining about the numerous plot holes on daytime television.

It will be very, very happy here.

And you can have the beastie back in a month's time, after you've written your book. Your Inner Editor, despite its incompatibility with rough drafts, is the perfect companion for the rewrite process. Because at that point, you will be giving it enough big-picture work to do that it won't have the time or energy to exhaust you with nitpicky comments about every comma and contraction.

So here's the deal I'm proposing: I'll take that heavy, anxious Inner Editor off your hands for four weeks. No charge. And in exchange, you promise to write your novel in a high-velocity, take-no-prisoners, anything-goes style that would absolutely horrify it.

All you need to do is touch the "Take My Inner Editor" button below, and a small, invisible team of humane, editor-removal specialists will be dispatched from the spine of this book to collect the thing for the kennel.

Since your Inner Editor will be led away within a few seconds of you pressing the button, don't touch it until you're ready. Take a few moments if you need to. Once your Inner Editor is safely in our kennels (and well out of earshot), we'll run through the last few things you need to know before setting out on your trip.

← PRESS HERE

Okay, with that behind us, let's get ready to go. I have just three final requests before we get started.

1. Please take this challenge very seriously. • You've signed the Month-Long Novelist Agreement and Statement of Understanding. Now see it through. Set regular writing goals, and stick to them. Your brain may be telling you it's time to turn off the computer and go to bed. But the human brain, if left to its own devices, would spend its entire adult life napping in front of the television. Ignore your brain. Toughen up. Keep your butt in that chair until you've bagged the day's quota. It's the only way you'll ever survive to see the finish line.

2. Do not take any of this very seriously. • Writing a novel in a month is utterly ridiculous, an undertaking for fools and those who don't know any better. Thankfully, we belong to the latter camp, which makes us dangerously powerful writers. Liberated from the constraints of constructing a pretty and proper novel, we are free to run, naked and whooping, through the valleys of our imaginations.

This month, your story will achieve an at-times frightening force and velocity. Go with it. Write wildly, joyfully, in huge and bounding strokes. Was that last page the worst thing you've ever written? Maybe. Does it matter? Nope. All words are good words this month. Follow tangents. Change directions at will. Stay loose. Make messes. Laugh at it all. You are doing something weird and wonderful here, and none of it will go on your permanent record.

3. Know that you have done all of this before. • If there's one thing humans excel at, it's telling tales. Our narrative voices have been honed through years of conversation and gossipy emails. We know how to string audiences along, slowly deploying just enough of the juicy bits to keep them hanging. The ability to braid together life experiences in a compelling way is part of our birthright.

Throughout the month, you'll find yourself drawing on strengths and abilities you didn't realize you possessed. There will be excruciatingly difficult days, sure. But the skills and tools to get you through the hard times are already within you. You've been writing a novel your whole life. This month is just the time when you finally get it down on paper.

Okay, let's do a final check, and then you're ready to head off. Do you have:

- [ ] A magical writing totem or two?
- [ ] Your reference book?
- [ ] Music to write to?
- [ ] Snacks, drinks, and luxury pampering supplies?

Then you're ready to go. Take a deep breath, head over to that word-processing device, and turn it on.

I think there's a novel that's been waiting a long time to meet you.

Week One Issues →

At the start of each week, we'll take a look at some of the time-specific hurdles, junctions, and way stations that you'll be passing during those seven days on your way to 50,000 words. This week, we'll look at the conundrums related to the first sentence, the first time you save your manuscript, and the end of the first chapter.

It Was the Best of Times, It Was the Worst of Times: Writing the Ideal First Sentence

The first sentence is, in many ways, a perfect microcosm of your novel. Meaning you're probably worrying way too much about it.

Your first sentence does not need to reflect the dynamic character of your novel. It is not an oracle or bellwether for how well the month will go, nor is it a predictor of the beautiful or horrendous

TIMING IS EVERYTHING: OPTIMIZING YOUR NOVELING TIME BY FINDING YOUR GOLDEN HOURS

One of the greatest lessons you'll learn over the next four weeks is that it's possible to churn out inspired prose regardless of how tired and unhappy you are when you sit down to write.

That said, everyone has certain hours of the day where the brain is just better-oiled than others. Finding out when these juicy hours fall, and spending as much time at the keyboard during them, will offer a tremendous boost to your book. These golden hours vary from person to person: Mine happen to run from about 9:00 a.m., when the coffee first hits, to 1:00 p.m., when all I want to do is crawl under my desk and fall asleep. If your most alert, creative hours occur in the morning (while you're at work or school), you can still make a point of exploiting them on weekends. Ditto for the night owls who just start hitting their stride around 3:00 a.m.

And whenever you have an especially challenging scene to write, try putting it off until you can have a go at it from within your golden hours' friendly synaptic confines.

prose that will follow it. It's simply a friendly announcement from your fingers to your brain that it best stop working on other things and get its butt down to your novel.

In this way, your first sentence is really just a set of chimes decorating the door of your novel, more of a ceremonial marker of a threshold than any sort of purposeful item. So go ahead and start the book off with whatever left-field image or statement occurs to you.

In my novels, I like to start with something storytelly to loosen my mental muscles. Past winners have included: "Okay, the story starts like this . . ." Or, "Crap. Time to start the novel. Okay, well, I guess it opens on . . ." Or, most originally, "Once upon a time . . ."

At some point, your first sentence will be reshaped into a beautifully inviting calling card for your book. Happily, that time is still at least a month away. For now you should go with whatever strikes your fancy.

Knowing When to Bring the Curtains Down: Ending Chapters

As you write this week, you will likely come up against another very good initial question. Namely: When am I supposed to end a chapter?

Some sections contain clear cut-points—a character going to bed, for example, or stepping in front of a bus—but early in the writing process, when you're not exactly sure where your story is headed, your chapters are bound to be lopsided and distinctly unchapterlike, with some going on for thirty pages and others barely managing to last an entire sentence.

This is totally fine. Later in the month you'll begin carving out well-paced, evenly allocated chapters as you find your book's rhythm. For now, you can't have too many or too few, so chapterize at will, captain.

Week One Tips →

Throughout the next four chapters, we'll also take a look at some strategies that will come in especially handy in dealing with each week's particular challenges. Week One's tips center on leveraging the adrenaline rush of the first few days, avoiding the pernicious desire to self-edit as you write, creating a convenient home for your castaway thoughts, and maintaining momentum by keeping your story a mystery to those around you.

Ride the Momentum

The first week of writing is an explosively productive creative period. With good reason. Your imagination, consigned to enjoying and analyzing other people's creative efforts from the sidelines for so long, has finally been asked to send some ideas down onto the field for its own shot at the big time.

Your imagination, understandably, is going to get a little over-excited at its moment in the spotlight. So rather than solemnly suggesting an orderly progression of characters and story ideas, it will send an entire screaming busload of contenders careening onto the field, where they will collide with each other, knock over the marching band, and wreak unholy havoc on the turf.

This is an unforgettable moment, and you should ride it for all it's worth. Even if you don't know *exactly* how you're going to fit those five ninjas into your courtroom drama, hey, they've arrived. And they want to be in the book. So put them in there. Inevitably they'll do *something* for the plot. If their performance doesn't end up meriting their inclusion, you can always clip them out later.

That's the beauty of novel writing: A panoply of strange characters, spread out over cities or continents, will somehow end up banding together midbook to construct your plot. You probably won't see how this will happen early in the writing process, and you shouldn't worry about it yet. Your role as a writer in Week One is just to continue to wave all of these players down onto the field, and then write like hell to keep up with them.

KEEPING BETH FROM BERTHA: AVOIDING THE DREADED "NAME DRIFT"

As you christen each of your characters, be sure to jot their names down on an easily accessed piece of paper or computer file. You'll be amazed how easily a Mike can become a Mick (who will in turn become a Matt) without some handy visual reminder to keep all the identities straight.

BURNING THE MIDNIGHT ALTOID

Between work, school, family, and errands, the only time many of us have to get writing done are the quiet, pre-bed hours. Writers in their teens or twenties will have no trouble handling an occasional regimen of burning the candle at both ends. For us older writers, though, all-nighters are out of the question, and we'll need all the help we can get to keep from ruining the romantic late-night writing tableau by falling asleep at the keyboard.

Happily, there are a host of tricks you can use to turn the barren wastelands of exhausted evenings into productive writing oases. As you might expect, coffee drinkers do very well in the month-long noveling arena, and java junkies will likely find themselves brewing up thick pots of the stuff at all hours. Green teas, along with the South American herb yerba mate, also make great coffee substitutes for those who don't like coffee's flavor. For those unfortunate souls who become jittery zombies when dosed with caffeine, there are a host of equally powerful stimulants to make the brain sparkle, even in the wee hours. Some of the best include:

→ **Fresh air:** Crack a window or, better still, go sit outside on the front steps for a few minutes. This is especially reviving if you're noveling in winter months. Plant lovers can drag all of their little friends into their writing room to create a low-intensity oxygen bar.

→ **Peppermints:** A NASA-funded study showed that the oils of the peppermint plant increased alertness by 30 percent and decreased fatigue by 15 percent. Peppermint tea, peppermint candies, and peppermint oil all work fine.

→ **Spicy foods:** These work in essentially the same way as a whiff of peppermint, giving your trigeminal nerve a reviving jolt. Can anyone say "chips and salsa"?

→ **Sunlight:** This one takes a little planning, as sunlight tends to be relatively hard to come by at 11:00 p.m. The good news is that sunlight absorbed during the day—even on cloudy days—has been shown to elevate moods long after the sun goes down.

With so much great input coming your way, Week One is a fantastic time to build up a comfortable word-count lead. If you're not exhausted after writing the day's 1,667-word quota, keep going to 2,000. And then to 3,000. On the first weekend of your mission, try to rack up 5,000 words if you can. You'll be *very* thankful for the cushion when you arrive at Week Two. Which is when things, ahem, change a little.

Don't Delete, *Italicize*

Even during anything-goes Week One, you'll write a few things that you recognize right away just don't fit in the book. Maybe you took a character in a new direction and didn't like it, or had a conversation that revealed too much too soon.

When you write these things, whether they constitute a sentence, a paragraph, or an entire chapter, do not cut them. All words you write on your novel, no matter how misshapen or ill-advised, still represent crucial steps toward the 50,000-word finish line.

Rather than deleting these passages, put them in italics. Italics, in its skinny, slanted way, is the next best thing to nonexistence. And your words are already flagged for evaluation when your Inner Editor returns for the rewrite phase later.

If even the sight of your italicized miscues distracts you to the point of writing inactivity, you can take things a step further and change the color of the italicized text from black to white, rendering it invisible (yet still word-countable). At the end of the month, you can use the "select all" command to turn the entire draft back to black, and go in with your editing scalpel to make your excisions.

Start a Novel Notes File

As you write, you'll come up with a number of jokes, plot developments, and bits of dialogue that would be great to slip into the book at some point in the future. While your magical noveling notebook is still the main go-to for breakthroughs and discoveries you have while out exploring the real world, you should start a Novel Notes file on your computer, and have it open at all times while writing.

Sensitive People: Keep the Story to Yourself

We all want people around us to love our work-in-progress, and getting a laugh or a "Wow, I can't wait to read that!" can boost morale in a wonderful way. There's no harm in reading a few paragraphs to loved ones, or posting short bits online.

But even sharing a small amount of your work-in-progress will encourage you to spend some amount of time editing and revising the text so it's presentable. This will sound a high-pitched whistle that only your Inner Editor can hear, and it will begin rattling the bars of its kennel, desperate to get out and "help" you.

That is the kind of help you can do without.

Also, if you're thin-skinned, anything short of rapturous acclaim will make you worry about the quality of your work and the direction your story has taken. Even worse, your audience might misinterpret your sharing as a request for constructive criticism. At that point, the self-doubt *really* kicks in, because you've replaced your own Inner Editor with someone else's.

If you are easily swayed by the reactions of others, resist the temptation to share your work-in-progress. After you've finished the entire first draft, you can show it to whoever you like and get the feedback you'll need to improve it.

Actually, come to think of it, you also should resist the temptation to share your work-in-progress with *yourself* as well. Rereading parts of your first draft while writing is like doubling back and rerunning portions of a marathon midrace. The best plan is to keep moving forward, allowing yourself only an orienting glimpse back into your story when you set out on each day's writing mission.

WRITING THE THINGS THAT SCARE YOU
BY GAYLE BRANDEIS

If you have allergies, you know about scratch tests. You go to the allergist's office, and they inject your back with a bunch of different substances in categories like "Home," "Mold," "Food," "Trees," then wait to see which ones bubble into itchy welts.

Before you begin your novel, I want you to do something similar. No, you don't have to inject yourself with anything, and you probably won't get itchy, other than (I hope) the itch to write. What I want you to do is create a list of things you have strong reactions to—things that make your heart pound, your breath catch. I've found that when we write about the things that scare us, the things that we cringe against, our writing comes to deeper, fuller life.

Here are some categories for your literary scratch test:

- **My deepest fears.**
- **Social/political issues that break my heart.**
- **Places that repel me.**
- **The qualities that annoy me most in people.**
- **Smells and tastes that make me sick.**
- **Objects that creep me out.**

Now list at least five things for each category, and be as specific as possible. If you're ever feeling lost as you move forward with your novel, turn to your list and see which items elicit the biggest reaction, which ones freak you out in the most visceral way, then throw one or two of them into a scene with your characters. When you inject your own fears into the world of your story, when you allow yourself to enter your own shadow, your own darkness on the page, your story will take you on a more mythic journey than you could ever imagine—and you just may end up slaying some of your own dragons in the process.

May you scratch your every creative itch this month and beyond.

GAYLE'S NANOWRIMO NOVELS INCLUDE *SELF STORAGE, THE BOOK OF LIVE WIRES,* AND *SEED BOMBS.*

SARA GRUEN'S HIGH-VELOCITY NOVELING SECRETS

Movies are one of the best ways to decompress after a heady day of noveling. And one of my all-time favorite movie moments was watching the big-screen adaptation of Sara Gruen's mega-best-selling novel, *Water for Elephants*. That book, along with Sara's *Flying Changes* and *Ape House*, began in NaNoWriMo.

I checked in with Sara to see how she approaches her month-long drafts, and see what tips she had for writers heading out on their own creative treks.

When it comes to planning, it turns out Sara deliberately leaves some big holes in her story. "Typically I know the setting and the crisis," she says, "but I don't know the ending. And while I may think I know the characters going in, they always turn into very different people."

The hardest part about NaNoWriMo for her? Shutting off her Inner Editor and leaving all that rushed, imperfect prose on the page. "I know my first drafts are sloppy and need a ton of work," she says, "so just pushing through to the end is a major milestone."

With two best-sellers under her belt, I wondered if Sara still faced those moments where her work-in-progress felt like a total disaster. "All the time!" she says. "Each book is a roller coaster, and the highs and lows get more extreme for me with each one."

After NaNoWriMo, Sara keeps plugging away, adding another 50,000 words or so before tackling her revision. It takes her anywhere from nine months to two years to get from the NaNoWriMo finish line to a completed novel, and she relies on outside help to know how much work her story needs. "I have a few close, trusted readers who would tell me if my book was awful, so I believe them if they say it's good. I also believe them if they say I need to fix something, even if it means rewriting half the book."

The tip that's inspired Sara through all her years of high-velocity first drafts? "I'm still a firm believer in the seat-of-the-pants in the seat-of-the-chair advice," she says. "Show up for work, because the novel will not write itself."

Week One Exercises →

In addition to week-specific issues and tips, we'll also highlight a couple of exercises you can do to help keep your creative juices flowing.

"Tell Me about Your Uncle": Fleshing Out Characters through Random Conversations with Friends and Strangers

As any psychologist will tell you, truth is definitely stranger than fiction. If you're having trouble coming up with interesting attributes and histories for your characters, tap into the millions of hilarious, wonderful characters already in orbit around you. Grab your notebook, call a friend, and ask them to tell you everything they know about their strangest relative.

Even some of the most mundane stories ("I had an uncle who wore flannel shirts every single day of his life. He used to sneak bologna into the zoo to throw to the gibbons because he always thought they looked too skinny.") will often spark ideas about potential characters and stories.

This tactic also works well with strangers, especially cute ones who will no doubt be impressed by this crazy novel project. So the next time you're in line at the grocery store and someone catches your eye, take out your pen and go harvest their family. You'll net a tremendous haul of anecdotes that you can steal for your story, and they'll come away telling their friends about the hot writer they met in the checkout line.

I, Couch Potato

Ah, the rigors of homework. The second exercise this week involves watching TV. Pick any show you enjoy. Just make sure it's fictional, and make sure it isn't one that you love so much that you will lose track of the assignment. Which is this: Sit down in front of the boob tube, put on your thinking cap, and watch critically.

Whatever show you've chosen, from *The Simpsons* to *CSI*, keep an eye out for how the writers tackle the same challenges you're facing in your novel: trying to fit a lot of story into a little time. Most TV shows have a main plot garlanded by one or two subplots. Some give each of the show's main characters a role in processing a single plot.

How many plots does your show juggle? How long does it wait before introducing the Central Problem? How and when does it use foreshadowing to let the viewers know what's coming? How is the story divvied up between the many characters? Is the outcome predictable? If you liked some aspect of the show's story, are there structural devices—pacing, narration, anything—you can steal from it?

Dissecting a TV show is a great way to help you see the tropes of storytelling laid bare. If you're hungering for more storytelling models, pop in a DVD or fire up your stream of choice and watch how the same conflicts are handled in a movie. As embarrassing as it is to report—and this secret does not leave the pages of this book—I modeled the pacing of one of my favorite month-long novels on the animated movie *Antz* and a rerun of *Cheers*.

Sigh.

Nobel Prize Committee, here I come, right? But whatever works, works. And TV shows and movies are a treasure trove of storytelling wisdom, both good and bad.

WEEK ONE RECAP

REPUTATION:

→ The easygoing opening to a bonkers month.

GOALS:

→ Write 11,600 words by the end of the week.

→ Introduce your characters and their worlds.

DO:

→ Begin anywhere.

→ Try to get ahead of word-count pace.

→ Suspend judgment and give yourself plenty of room to play, explore, and make interesting messes.

DON'T:

→ Delete anything.

→ Feel like each chapter has to be "right" before you move on to the next one.

→ Be dismayed if your prose is much worse than the novels you love—they all started out as deeply flawed first drafts too!

REMEMBER:

→ Editing is for next month. Retrain your brain to go for quantity instead of quality (which, strangely, will net you both).

TIPS FROM THE TRENCHES:
NANOWRIMO WINNERS ON WEEK ONE

What It Feels Like

"The best thing about Week One is the promise. Your novel could be anything—it could be the next international best seller, it could be a future classic, it could be the first step on the road toward your glittering literary career. The worst thing is the little voice in your head that tells you it will be terrible."
—EMILY HOGARTH, FIVE-TIME NANOWRIMO WINNER FROM WELLS, UNITED KINGDOM

"One of the biggest thrills of Week One comes when you first start to see the words slowly piling up, and it hits you—this could really happen. You could actually write a book in a month!"
—LAUREN COFFIN, EIGHT-TIME NANOWRIMO WINNER FROM BOSTON, MASSACHUSETTS

"You're meeting all your characters, going on a new journey, and knowing that great things are in store. The worst thing is staring at that 50,000 mark and realizing that, however far you've come in that first week, you still have so far to go."
—LUCY RALSTON, FOUR-TIME NANOWRIMO WINNER FROM ATHENS, GEORGIA

How to Rock It

"For Day One, stay up at midnight and write. Write at least 200–300 words if you can."
—PATRICIA PINTO, SIX-TIME NANOWRIMO WINNER FROM PETALING JAYA, MALAYSIA

"Describe all of your characters in loving and extremely wordy detail when you introduce them. "
—ERIN ALLDAY, TWELVE-TIME NANOWRIMO WINNER FROM BERKELEY, CALIFORNIA

"Have the arc of your first chapter ready to go, so on Day One you can just dive in."
—JASON SNELL, SIX-TIME NANOWRIMO WINNER FROM MILL VALLEY, CALIFORNIA

"Breathe."
—JACKI DRAYCOTT, FIVE-TIME NANOWRIMO WINNER FROM BLACKPOOL, UNITED KINGDOM

"As a seat-of-the-pants writer, I like to spend Week One creating my world. I don't worry about setting the plot in motion right away—I just describe every facet of the character's world as it comes to me, from their relationship with their mother to their favorite pizza."
—**DENTON FROESE,** NINE-TIME NANOWRIMO WINNER FROM MEDICINE HAT, CANADA

"Don't freak out when you can't hit 1,667 words every day. There will be some days you can barely hit 500, and other days you will find yourself pushing past 3,000."
—**JONATHAN FERGUSON,** ONETIME NANOWRIMO WINNER FROM NAIROBI, KENYA

"Split up your writing sessions. I aim for half my goal in the mornings before work, and the other half after office hours. If you have a commute, start to make use of it."
—**MAY CHONG,** THREE-TIME NANOWRIMO WINNER FROM PETALING JAYA, MALAYSIA

"Week One is when I find my normal exercise routine to be extremely important. I cannot emphasize enough how many plot lines, story epiphanies, and random bits of character knowledge have come to me while on a run."
—**ELIZABETH GREGG,** THREE-TIME NANOWRIMO WINNER FROM OAKLAND, CALIFORNIA

"If you can write during every day of Week One, even if it's only for ten minutes each day, you are much more likely to finish your novel."
—**STEVEN HOFFMAN,** TWO-TIME NANOWRIMO WINNER FROM BUFFALO, NEW YORK

"Week One is the week you establish your good NaNo habits! Be especially brutal about waking up 30 minutes early."
—**IMAAN ASRI,** FOUR-TIME NANOWRIMO WINNER FROM KUALA LUMPUR, MALAYSIA

"Don't try to pace yourself in Week One; take that enthusiasm and run with it. I usually get about a third of my total word count in Week One, which really helps when life catches up with me in later weeks."
—**PATIENCE VIRTUE,** THREE-TIME NANOWRIMO WINNER FROM ALBANY, OREGON

"Save often. Nothing is worse than losing a few hundred words because you forgot to save."
—**OLIVIA COACKLEY,** THREE-TIME NANOWRIMO WINNER FROM PLEASANTON, CALIFORNIA

"Never be discouraged by other people's word counts."
—**SYAHIRA SHARIF,** THREE-TIME NANOWRIMO WINNER FROM PETALING JAYA, MALAYSIA

6. WEEK TWO: STORM CLOUDS, PLOT FLASHES, AND THE RETURN OF REALITY

Dear Writer,

One week in, and we're right on target: Our homes are a mess, our friends are annoyed, and our bosses have started casting suspicious, sidelong glances at us as they walk by our cubicles.

It's been a promising beginning. In the last seven days alone, you've written a small novella's worth of people and places. And you've felt the sexy click of your imagination as it locks on target, the muscly thrill of your badass creative self rolling up its sleeves and wading into the fray.

There's much to celebrate. But, sadly, there's also some bad news on the way. The *No Plot? No Problem!* team of literary meteorologists has radioed an urgent message back from the noveling front. There's a storm rolling in from the west—a black howler of a tempest. And it's headed your way.

Welcome to Week Two. If you brought a poncho, now would be a good time to get it out.

The storm will likely break in three or four days, exactly at the point when the novelty of the event starts to fade, and your book starts getting more demanding.

Cue thunder. Cue lightning. And cue some big-time writerly grumpiness.

Those first thunderclaps mark an essential turning point in novel writing; it's the place where the cast has been introduced, the stage has been set, and everything is primed for the story to unfold. Having reached this stage, most novelists would pat themselves on the back and head off to Majorca for a month to celebrate their accomplishments.

But because of the pressing time frame, you barely have time to catch your breath, much less catch a plane. For better or worse, the next great stage—plot building—is upon us.

Yep. You've wrapped up the exposition, and now something book-like has to happen. Someone needs to fall in love. Or get amnesia. Or go on a road trip. But who? And how?

The questions just keep piling up, and your first impulse will likely be to chuck the whole thing and go back to the blissful life you led before this five-headed literary monster began devouring all your free time.

As you write your way through the next seven days, know that Week Two hurts so bad because you're making huge strides in your book, solving a year's worth of plot and character problems in one overcaffeinated week.

The answers will come. Just keep at it, and before you know it, Week Two will be a distant memory. The sun will be shining again, the way will be clear, and the writing will become fun once more.

And Week Three! Oh, don't get me started about the wonders of Week Three. There are some amazing things on your literary horizons. The kinds of breakthroughs that will make you laugh and cry and shake your head pityingly at friends and family members who wasted this month on empty pursuits like conversation, bathing, and sleep.

The only way to get to that self-righteously pitying stage, though, is by hurling yourself directly into the eye of Week Two's storms. Now is the time to batten down the hatches and throw yourself into your story with everything you've got.

You've made such great progress, writer. And the best is just around the bend.

Week Two Issues ⟶

Still No Plot? Still No Problem.

If you already know the intricacies of how your novel is going to unfold, Week Two is the point when you'll begin putting your fiendish plan into action. The players are in position, and it's time to tip that first domino, to open the story's throttle and watch it speed ahead.

If you still don't know what your characters are doing in your book, Week Two is the point when you should panic.

Hee hee.

Just kidding.

Having a shaky, hazy, or problematic plot heading into Week Two is absolutely fine, and is a predicament common to many month-long novelists. I guarantee that if you meet your word count quota over the next seven days, you'll have a much, much clearer idea of what your book is about by the end of the week.

As I said before, plot is just the movement of your characters through time, over the course of your book. If you're still not clear on your book's plot, the best thing you can do for your story is to really let your characters move this week. Give them space to show parts of themselves they may have kept hidden in the first seven days. Encourage them to act out, to indulge their desires, no matter how zany or destructive those desires may be. Allow change, and plot will happen.

Character Coups

If you're have trouble seeing a possible plot in your novel, one of the problems may be your growing boredom or disenchantment with your main characters. If you've been noticing that, despite your best intentions, the camera lens of your book tends to drift to the incidental members of the cast—the best friend, the coworker, or the family iguana, say—it may be a sign that the book would be better recentered in their orbit.

Demoting your hero from savior to sidekick and promoting some of your supporting characters to starring roles happens a lot in the figuring-it-out-as-you-go world of month-long novel-writing.

SO YOU WANT TO START OVER: A WARNING ABOUT DIVORCING YOUR NOVEL AND RUNNING OFF WITH A NEW STORY

Everyone, at some point, sees their novel as a lost cause. The characters are one-dimensional. The plot isn't going anywhere. The language is abysmal. For month-long novelists, this moment typically occurs in Week Two, when the general unhappiness about the hours you've been keeping and the challenges of plot improvisation make even the most promising story look like a disaster.

The thing to remember even in the darkest moments is that there *is* something great and workable in your story. Rather than starting over entirely, the best approach is usually to focus on the book's strengths—the characters or parts of the story line you are enjoying—and let the story take off from there.

Before you do anything drastic, sit down and think about story directions and exciting imbroglios that might spin off from your new potential protagonist(s). If you come up with a few good ones, or find yourself salivating at the thought of letting someone else take the spotlight from the dullard currently narrating your story, a character coup may be for you.

Falling Behind and the Key to the VIP Lounge

Okay, let's be honest: There will be days in this wild escapade when you're just not feeling it. When your brain has checked out and neglected to leave a forwarding address, and it's all you can do to get the food from the dinner plate to your mouth before you collapse, asleep, at the table.

These days will come more often than you might like in Week Two, and to avoid getting overwhelmed, now is a great time to give yourself the occasional novel-free night. Even if you're behind on your word count, taking a night off to replenish those overtaxed synapses will likely end up boosting your productivity in the long run.

Whenever you do skip a writing day, though, be sure to make up the words within a couple of days. As you know all too well by now, every day you skip steers you another 1,667 words off course. Accumulate three or four wordless days in a row, and the book becomes less of a spontaneous creative experiment and more of a ten-round grudge match between you and your hulking literary deficit.

Staying on pace, on the other hand, grants you access to the *No Plot? No Problem!* VIP Writer's Lounge. This swank place is the finest writer's nook in the world; the coffee is free, the people are friendly and inspiring, and the chairs are all orthopedic custom jobbies with expansive lumbar support.

The VIP Lounge is an ideal refuge from some of the rough weather that will be passing over your novel in Week Two. Do what you can to haul yourself up into its ritzy confines, but remember that *staying reasonably sane is the week's ultimate goal.* If you have to take on some word debt to keep burnout at bay, do so. You can always set up residency in the VIP Lounge next week.

Week Two Tips →

"Don't Get It Right, Get It Written": Making Decisions in Week Two

When asked for the most important piece of writing insight she's ever received, Edgar Award–winning mystery writer Julie Smith quoted some advice from her newspaper days. "Don't get it right, Smith," a gruff editor had told her. "Get it written."

That advice looms large over Week Two, and it is something to keep in mind as you decide what to do with all these characters that have taken up residency in your book.

The variety of directions a book can take are a little daunting. Do you kill someone off? Give someone amnesia? Send the lot of them on a road trip?

In deciding what should happen next in your book, know that all plot points lead to the same happy place: getting a complete draft of your novel done. You aren't shooting for perfection here; you're just exploring the outer reaches of your imagination, and building a book one day at a time. Don't worry about getting it right this week. That will come in the revisions. This week, your goal is just to get it written.

The Mind Is Willing, the Immune System Weak: Avoiding Pathogens and Other Enemies of Fine Literature

Colds, flus, and other opportunistic viruses are the failed writers of the microbe world. They have a good story to tell, but they lack the drive, discipline, and typing appendages to get the stories down on paper. Like most stymied creative types, they'll stop at nothing to bring down the brave few who dare to seize their dreams.

Because of this, you should guard your health very, very carefully from this point forward. Especially if you've been sleeping four hours a night and eating most of your meals at Taco Bell.

Wash your hands with soap every time you pass a faucet. Eat as many fruits and vegetables as you can stomach. Start stirring vitamin C into your whiskey shots. And if you are in a public space—such as a restaurant or an airplane cabin—and someone begins coughing, flee immediately. Your body will thank you, and your novel will thank you, too.

The Check-In: Staying in Touch When You Don't Have Time to Write

On days when you don't have the time or energy for a full writing session, you can help keep your word debt low with quick writing

OBSESSIVE COUNTING DISORDER

Psychologists have a term to describe people who perform small gestures and rituals over and over again uncontrollably: obsessive-compulsive disorder. Month-long novelists who don't already have OCD will be getting a crash course in the mental illness thanks to the "word count" feature built into writing programs. Nothing is more alluring than pulling up a tally of your progress as you type, and you'll likely find yourself checking your word count after every paragraph. Assessing your progress after every couple of lines, though, is like checking the odometer every five minutes on a thousand-mile road trip—knowing how far you've gone does nothing to get you there faster, and it makes the journey seem interminably slow. One way to get around this is to structure your writing around units of time rather than numbers of words, and then make word-counting a reward you earn at the end of each noveling session.

sessions I call Check-Ins. These are noveling quickies where you just poke your head into your novel for twenty minutes or so, add a pinch of color here, an embellishment there, and then call it a night after 500 words or so.

It may seem like a pitiful drop in the bucket, but every word you write is one less you'll have to tackle the next day. The main point of a Check-In, though, is to help you maintain a creative connection to your book so your imagination will continue to nibble away at the story until you sit down for the next full-blown write-in.

Week Two Exercises →

Getting On Your Case: How Friends and Family Can Help Plot Your Novel

In the business school world, the teaching of proper management is partly done through nifty things called business cases. These are swashbuckling tales of the exploits of managers and employees at companies where change (or the lack thereof) is threatening the well-being of the organization. Business cases lead students through the who and where of the story right up to the point when a strategic decision needs to be made to decide the fate of the company. And then the MBA students must debate what they'd do if they were in the CEO's or middle manager's shoes.

The same teaching aid that's transformed mild-mannered graduate students into ruthless, bloodthirsty entrepreneurs can also be harnessed to help you gain new insights on your book. This week, try making a business case out of your novel.

Here's how it works: Ask a couple of friends who enjoy the same kinds of books you do to meet with you for an hour. Then, once everyone's comfortable, hand out some scratch paper and pens, and explain the ground rules: You are going to give them a handful of characters, a setting, and a *veeery* vague story direction, and they are to tell you what should happen next.

Explain everything you know about your characters, one by one—where they work, who they love, what they're embarrassed by, and so on. Encourage your story students to jot down questions and ideas as they occur to them, but be sure to emphasize that this is a brainstorming session, not a test; there are no right or wrong story directions.

After you've completely described all of your characters and their connections to each other, your job is to get the conversational

CHEAP PADDING TECHNIQUES: EASY TRICKS FOR GETTING YOUR WORD COUNT UP WHEN YOU'RE FEELING DOWN

There will be times in your writing journey when you want to curl up and die. These moments will pass, but desperate times call for desperate measures, and there are a host of word-count-increasing tricks that well-seasoned month-long novelists use to help pad their novels (and warm their spirits) in these dark hours.

Here are some of the old standbys:

A stutter: Afflict one of your characters with a stutter, and it doubles their dialogue's girth. It also allows the supporting cast to spend several pages wondering in great, word-count bolstering detail about the sudden, mysterious onset of the speech impediment.

Temporary deafness: Everything from loud rock concerts to small deposits of earwax can temporarily render your character deaf, requiring everything said to him or her be repeated. And repeated. And repeated.

The dream sequence: Dreams might as well come with a sign that says, "Free words: Help yourself." The dream sequence (and its cousin, the hallucination) go on for as long as you like and don't have to make any sense whatsoever. It's the mother lode!

The citation: If your character can read, you can cite. Give your protagonist a copy of *Beowulf* and an annoying habit of reading poetry out loud on the long commute to work, and you've suddenly added thousands of words to your count. This also works with songs, newspaper articles, and—gulp—other novels.

The extended name: Okay, say your protagonist is named Jane. Every occurrence of Jane's name only nets you a single tick on the word counter. Now let's say you use the find-and-replace function on your word processor to change "Jane" to "Jane Marie." Presto! You've doubled your investment. This works especially well in fantasy novels, where a low-yield name like Hrudon can, with a single find-and-replace search, become "Hrudon, Son of Sankar, Prince and Overlord of Outer Cthandon."

De-hyphenate: Word-processing programs tend to count hyphenated words as a single unit. *Lily-livered* is just one word; "not-quite-as-potent-as-promised fungicide" counts, mysteriously, as only two words. Deleting your hyphens may lose you grammar points, but it will definitely gain you words when you're too tired to write any new ones.

ball rolling and then become invisible. Let your audience argue, debate, and build off one another's ideas as you take notes on everything they say. Even if you already know what will happen in your book, you'll get amazing insights on motivations, subplots, and other nefarious activities that might make your book more interesting.

When your focus group inevitably asks what you think should happen in the story, be sure to keep your ideas a mystery. As mentioned in Chapter 5, revealing your book's plot before it's written can end up sapping a lot of the joy from the writing process, especially if your focus group has a tepid reaction to it—or thinks it stinks. Just keep scribbling down notes and ideas, and let them know that all will be revealed when the book comes out in hardback.

FREE EMAIL BACKUPS

Computers, unfortunately, go belly-up all the time. If your writing device of choice isn't automatically archiving every precious word to the cloud, you can protect yourself from heartbreak by making email backups of your novel. Just email your novel to yourself as an attachment every few days, leaving the email unopened on the server until the next backup arrives. Hopefully you'll never need to access it, but just in case you do, it's there.

Inciting Plot Flashes

No one has better encapsulated the spirit of month-long noveling than five-time NaNoWriMo winner Rise Sheridan-Peters, who describes her approach to writing as follows: "I don't wait for my muse to wander by; I go out and drag her home by the hair."

With time being of the essence this month, any hairy hand-hold you can use to hurry your novel along should be exploited. And certain activities work much better than others to stimulate the copious "aha!" breakthrough moments you'll have during your noveling month. I call these moments "plot flashes," and, inconveniently, most of them occur while you're far away from a keyboard.

For me, common sites for plot flashes include hot showers, dance clubs, and long bike rides. For some reason, creative juices just percolate better when accompanied by routine, automatic motions. When I set out on my bike for a five-mile ride, I know that I'll come home with invaluable material I didn't have before. Which is also why I take a notebook and pen out every time I go dancing.

Other NaNoWriMo winners recommend walking a dog, jumping on a bed, and flitting around at the edge of sleep as possible doorways to plot flashes. Try all of these and more this week, and see if any help you unleash your imagination.

AN OBJECT IN MOTION

BY RACHAEL HERRON

Remember Isaac Newton's Law of Motion: An object in motion stays in motion. This is especially true in Week Two. You started off great guns last week. Now you're realizing that everything you're writing is not only trite, but boring and ugly too. Good for you! You're perfectly on track. Here are some of my favorite tricks to keep the words coming this week.

1. Do it first. Get up 30 minutes early (not that bad, right?) and get a good jump on the words before you even brush your teeth. The page won't mind your morning breath.

2. During those in-between moments (showering, driving) play with the plot in your brain. Ask yourself what is the most outlandish thing that could happen in the next scene. Then write that when you get back to the page.

3. If the story takes off, create what I call a virtual Post-it. Switch to upper-case, make yourself a note of what to fix in the *next* draft— MAKE BETTY A LION TAMER INSTEAD OF A LIBRARIAN—then just keep going, as if you'd already written Betty that way. Whatever you do, don't go back and rewrite anything now! If you start over and have Betty taming lions left and right, then learn at the end that she actually needed to be a deep-sea welder in order to solve the mystery, you've wasted both time and lions. Just keep writing fast and hard with no thought to the consequences. (Your subconscious is doing the hard work already, I promise. You'll be amazed.) Don't make it *good*, not yet. Just keep making it.

RACHAEL'S NANOWRIMO NOVELS INCLUDE **HOW TO KNIT A LOVE SONG, HOW TO KNIT A HEART BACK HOME,** AND **CORA'S HEART**.

WEEK TWO RECAP

REPUTATION:

→ The going gets tough.

GOALS:

→ Hit 25,000 words by week's end.

→ Get that plot in motion.

DO:

→ Make big change happen in your story.

→ Get your characters out of their comfort zones and take away the things they need most.

→ Let your cheerleaders contribute story ideas.

→ Write every day (even if you're only writing a few words).

→ Embrace ridiculous word-count padding tricks if your story has stalled.

DON'T:

→ Worry about ruining your story by taking it down the wrong path—as long as you're moving the story forward you're doing great. If you you've completely lost the heartbeat of your story, double back to the last place in the manuscript you loved, and begin again from there. (Don't delete the intervening words! You may need them later.)

REMEMBER:

→ You are a hero for doing this! Celebrate every word-count milestone with treats and rewards.

TIPS FROM THE TRENCHES:

NANOWRIMO WINNERS ON WEEK TWO

What It Feels Like

"In Week Two I usually realize I'm not writing the story I thought I was. I refuse to give up or start over, and I don't let it get me down. I just decide to go with the story that's happening and see what exciting new things I can discover in that world instead."
—PATIENCE VIRTUE, THREE-TIME NANOWRIMO WINNER FROM ALBANY, OREGON

"Think of Week Two as that teacher that pushed you to exhaustion only because s/he/it knew you had potential. Week Two is doing this for your own good."
—PAZ ALONSO, EIGHT-TIME NANOWRIMO WINNER FROM FRANKFURT AM MAIN, GERMANY

"Week Two is when I start panicking and changing the point of view. I advise paying a large member of your family to punch you in the throat whenever you change 'he' to 'I,' or vice versa."
—C. A. BRIDGES, SIX-TIME NANOWRIMO WINNER FROM ORANGE CITY, FLORIDA

"I spend most of Week Two staying up late and writing while sleep-deprived. When you have 2,000 words to finish before you can go sleep, you don't care if it's a bad idea for the main character and antagonist to sleep together. You just go with the flow and leave them to figure it out."
—HEATHER CAPRIO, ONE-TIME NANOWRIMO WINNER FROM KOKOMO, INDIANA

"It's a speed bump, not a brick wall."
—PAM GRAY, THREE-TIME NANOWRIMO WINNER FROM FORT THOMAS, KENTUCKY

How to Rock It

"Don't get stuck in exposition. Keep moving the story forward."
—NICOLE PALMBY, TWO-TIME NANOWRIMO WINNER FROM JACKSONVILLE, ILLINOIS

"Remind yourself that no one, I repeat, no one else is going to see this draft."
—SONIA RAO, FOUR-TIME NANOWRIMO WINNER FROM MUMBAI, INDIA

"During Week Two, your notebook is your best friend. When you write by hand, your brain works differently, and starting the days writing on paper can cure an indecisive imagination."
—**BEN BYRIEL,** ONE-TIME NANOWRIMO WINNER FROM VEJLE, DENMARK

"Tell other people about your novel. This is the point when things get tough, and talking about your novel and seeing other people get excited about your plot and your characters gets you excited again."
—**MALERIE ANDERSON,** SIX-TIME NANOWRIMO WINNER FROM ST. CLAIRSVILLE, OHIO

"Week Two: chocolate."
—**MELANIE MACEK,** FIVE-TIME NANOWRIMO WINNER FROM VICTORIA, TEXAS

"The more flexible you are, the more fun Week Two will be."
—**LESLEY MORGAN,** SIX-TIME NANOWRIMO WINNER FROM JOHNSON CITY, TENNESSEE

"Shrink your document window until it's only two lines tall to keep yourself from editing."
—**CHRIS OLINGER,** SEVEN-TIME NANOWRIMO WINNER FROM SAINT JOSEPH, MISSOURI

"No naps."
—**SABRINA PANETTA,** ONE-TIME NANOWRIMO WINNER FROM OTTOWA, CANADA

"Sometimes filler is what you need to get over Week Two hurdles. It can always be edited out later, but I've found that Week Two filler generally leads me to new and cool revelations about my story."
—**ALEXA SCHMIDT,** THREE-TIME NANOWRIMO WINNER FROM CINCINNATI, OHIO

"Writing each chapter in a different file is helpful. If the words are not on the screen, you can't edit them."
—**JAMIE PHILLIPS,** THREE-TIME NANOWRIMO WINNER FROM MANCHESTER, UNITED KINGDOM

"Outline a bit to be sure you know where the story is going and forge on."
—**KAYLA J. W. MARNACH,** FIVE-TIME NANOWRIMO WINNER FROM AUSTIN, TEXAS

"In Week Two, I always end the evening's writing session midsentence. Itching to finish that sentence will get my butt back in the chair tomorrow."
—**HEATHER MILLARD,** ONE-TIME NANOWRIMO WINNER FROM AUSTIN, TEXAS

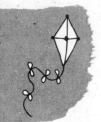

7. WEEK THREE: CLEARING SKIES, WARMER WEATHER, AND A JETPACK ON YOUR BACK

Dear Writer,

Welcome to Week Three! If last week was a stormy trek through ice-slicked mountain passes, Week Three is . . . well . . . nicer. Much nicer.

You've survived the most difficult part of the month. You still have a lot of work ahead, but the weather is more forgiving in Week Three, and the landscape softer. In the amiable confines of Week Three, gentle woodland creatures will begin appearing along the trail's edge, chanting your name, extending trays of nutrient-rich acorns and hollowed gourds brimming with Gatorade.

Or at least let's hope it's Gatorade.

Anyway, you should drink it all in. For this is the week when you begin to head downhill, when the beautiful, bucolic patch of earth called The End first becomes visible.

To get the most out of Week Three, there are two things you must do:

1. Lose any word debt you've accumulated. • If you fell behind in the grim slog of Week Two, you'll need to turn the productivity up a notch or three. To help enable this, the *No Plot? No Problem!* Employment Outreach Team has talked to your boss and brokered an agreement: You are henceforth allowed to novel on company time as long as nobody sees you doing it. (Under the terms of this agreement, you are also allowed to print out three copies of your finished novel on the office laser printer after everyone's gone home for the night.)

Whether you're writing from home or work, the month's timetable says you should have about 35,000 words by the end of this week. Ignore this timetable if you're far behind, focusing instead on hitting 30,000 words by the week's close. Whatever you do, though, breach the thirties by the dawn of Week Four.

2. Let gravity be your guide. • Things open up toward the middle of Week Three. The pitch of the noveling trail will shift beneath your feet, pointing you downhill at a steep slope. As your tale picks up speed, your first reaction may be to try to slow yourself, to steady your progress to an even and orderly pace.

Screw that. This is your time to fly.

Why? Because it's all going to start coming together this week. The ninjas your imagination randomly introduced in your courtroom drama back in Week One? They'll appear before the judge this week with some testimony that will turn the case upside down. The unstoppable zombies terrorizing the Coldplay concert will cease their marauding and begin to stagger as a single, piercing guitar note rings out over the crowd. And lowly bartender Ngiam Ton Boon at the Raffles Hotel in Singapore will reach out for gin and grab cherry brandy by mistake, changing the destiny of colonial-era alcoholics forever.

Week Three is when it all happens—when all those loose ends begin lashing themselves together as if by magic, creating connections and passageways through your novel that are both apt and effortless. Do well this week, and the novel is yours for the taking.

Week Three Issues →

Standing Halfway and Seeing the Future: Appraising Your Progress

You've officially crossed the continental divide of your novel month at this point. Congratulations! Now is a perfect moment for you to put word-count issues aside, size up your story, and figure out how close you are to The End.

In your guesstimation, are you:

- [ ] A) More than halfway through with your story?
- [ ] B) Exactly halfway through with your story?
- [ ] C) Less than halfway through with your story?

If you answered A or B, hallelujah. Great job. Continue full speed ahead. You're right on track with the pacing. If you're worried about running out of story before you hit 50,000 words, don't. For one, you probably have more wrapping up to do than you realize. And for two, a prologue, epilogue, and table of contents can always be conjured at the last minute to push your book over the edge of 50,000 words. There will be plenty for you to do if you reach the end of your novel before you reach the summit of your word count, so write quickly and with confidence.

If you answered C, though, we need to talk.

The goal here is to have your 49,999th and 50,000th words be "The" and "End." Not because your book will really be 50,000 words when you've had a chance to edit it. In fact, your story will probably gain an extra 10,000 to 50,000 words around its midsection during revisions.

No, you should try to write a complete story this month because you'll find the visionary work of creation becomes much, much more difficult after your #A30/31/50k deadline expires and your Inner Editor moves back home to live with you again.

For the next two weeks of writing, you will be bathing in dizzying amounts of momentum and literary moxie. You'll be closer to your characters than you may ever be again. All of which makes this the perfect time to nail down major decisions regarding plot and story line.

If you are still introducing characters and haven't yet sent them out in search of a plot, you should sit down and figure out where they're going now. What are the essential scenes you can focus on writing over the next two weeks so that you can have an entire story arc completed in two weeks' time? Skip ahead if you need to—using lots of in-text notes ("here is where the podiatrist will admit to Nancy that he's an alien") to keep track of the parts you're skipping over—and write only those scenes that move the story forward.

It can be disheartening to realize that you aren't going to be able to write every scene in your novel before the month ends, but I can tell you from experience that it is much easier to fill in connecting scenes and interludes during rewriting than it is to have to conceive

CAN I GIVE UP NOW?

No. You cannot give up now.

and write the final five chapters of a story after the month has ended. Avoid that by bending your story arc now so its tail end is pointing squarely at 50k.

"You're Still Working on that Thing?": When Support Networks Attack

Some NaNoWriMo participants are blessed with fanatical cheering sections and relentlessly supportive groups of friends and family who constantly ply them for details about their work-in-progress. These good-hearted folks make care packages stuffed with frozen pizzas and unmarked bills, and listen, enraptured, to the stories about life as an amateur novelist.

The other 99 percent of us have a somewhat less saintly support network. Our caregivers are dispensing bemused glances on good days, and are hurling our unwashed dishes at our heads on bad ones.

However, no matter how enthusiastic or disinterested your fans have been up till now, you'll probably notice an ebbing in their support this week.

It makes sense. Having a novel appear in your life so suddenly is like finding a baby—or a very small person convincingly dressed as a baby—on your doorstep. As you acclimate to the new presence in your life, old routines go out the window, and friends and family are inevitably pushed aside as you figure out how best to make room for the addition.

And, like a baby, a novel is largely a personal miracle; the tiny joys of your writing process usually won't resonate with other people, no matter how close you are to them.

Like many month-long writers, five-time winner Rise Sheridan-Peters finds this discrepancy between the joy of the book and the sorrow of friends and family especially pernicious in Week Three.

"I'm finally figuring out what the book is about," Rise says, "and everyone else in my life is counting the days until the book is done. I want them to sit and look at me raptly while I tell them that what's inside the suitcase turned out to be a forged reliquary with a fake saint's arm that's actually filled with designer drugs from a lab at MIT. They just want to know if we're ever going to eat another meal that didn't come in a bag with a plastic spork."

As you head into your third week of missed social engagements and poor performance on household chores, your friends and loved ones will be slowly realizing that if you were going to quit your book, you probably would have done so already. Which means another two weeks of closed doors and sporky dinners.

This may bring out a little grouchiness in your support team, mostly because they miss you. Or they at least miss the less annoying version of you who could sit through an entire movie without later telling them how many words you could have written in that two-hour period.

So, give a little love and understanding back, and assure your support networks that the thing is almost over.

Week Three Tips ➔

Activating the 6,000-Word Jetpack Under Your Seat

Tremendous come-from-behind victories have been a part of month-long noveling since the dawn of the sport. One of the easiest ways to go from out-of-contention to head-of-the-pack is by harnessing the power of 6,000-word days. These are much easier to pull off than you might imagine.

Here is a step-by-step guide to turning on your noveling jetpack:

☑ 1) Pick a Saturday or Sunday when you have approximately two-hour pockets of free time spread throughout the morning, afternoon, and evening.

☑ 2) Wake up early and have a large, healthy breakfast. Or some coffee and a cigarette, whichever is easiest.

☑ 3) Do three 30-minute writing sessions in a row, separated by 10-minute stretching/wrist-shaking/fetal-position-holding and complaining breaks.

☑ 4) Go have fun, and come back and repeat the same 3/30/10 schedule feat after lunch.

☑ 5) Do something else, and after dinner and some post-meal loafing, head to the computer and do another three 30-minute sessions.

☑ 6) At this point, you will have added 6,000 words to your tally, and can go to sleep dreaming of friendly agents bringing oversized advance checks to your door.

To exponentially increase the power of your jetpack, follow this regimen two days in a row. You will be floored by how much more lovable the world is when you add 12,000 words to your count over one weekend.

Out of Sight But Not Out of Mind: Banishing the Last Traces of Your Inner Editor

News from your Inner Editor! I just dropped by the kennel, and your Inner Editor is doing very well in your absence. While I was there, it was in the middle of correcting the pitch and pronunciation of a group of elementary-school carolers who had come by to spread good cheer.

I've never seen an editor so happy.

Despite your IE's contented distance, you may still be feeling its presence this week in the form of writing or creative blocks. If you are feeling stymied at Week Three, you were probably cursed with a more dictatorial Inner Editor than most. Here are some ways for you to cope with this style-cramping, book-blocking situation.

1. Break things. • Don't break real-world things (which tend to be expensive), but things in your novel. Your Inner Editor has long served the role of an overly protective parent. Now that your parent is out of town, it's time you leveraged those lessons from cinematic classics like *Risky Business* and *Sixteen Candles*: It's time to throw a party and trash the house.

Pick out a character that's been causing you no end of grief, and do something big and reckless with them. Have them exiled out of the story or get swallowed by a wormhole while waiting for the bus.

If you've hit a standstill in your efforts to bring two obviously perfect romantic leads together, kill one of them. Your readers won't see it coming, and in figuring out how to fix the mess you've just made of your story, you'll give your imagination the kind of fertile improvisational environment it needs to thrive.

2. Make a pact with yourself to eventually destroy all evidence that this novel ever existed. ● Part of your blockage may be the fact that you're already worrying about what people are going to say about your rough draft. This is an unnecessary worry, as everyone's first drafts are crappy, but you can address the worry directly by figuring out how you'll destroy your novel as soon as it's finished. Will you print it out, then burn it on the barbecue grill? Or bury the thing in the woods by the light of a full moon?

Once you absolutely remove from your mind the possibility that anyone else will read your work, you'll likely find yourself enjoying the writing process much more. Also, destroying your novel before anyone reads it will give you a sexy allure that's part Zen letting-go and part Jimi Hendrix writhing over his flaming Telecaster.

3. Go small. ● If you've stopped writing because you can't shake the feeling that all of your plot directions are unworthy, give your plotting brain a break by focusing on things that *won't* advance the story. Write 2,000 words about a sign dangling from a hotdog stand across the street from your protagonist's house. Spend pages describing the perfume your love interest wears, and why it's exactly the wrong thing for her. Write around the periphery of your story. Write beside or below your story. But whatever you do, just keep writing. Even if you spend the next couple of days writing background material, you'll have built a hell of a great nest for your story when you find your groove again.

GUEST PEP TALK

LOVING YOUR CHARACTERS, EVEN THE RUBBISH ONES
BY ELIZABETH HAYNES

This is my traditional slump week. My tip for Week Three, if your plot starts to falter, is to look closely at your characters.

By the halfway stage, most of my protagonists have become real. Even, worryingly, the socially phobic genius psychopath has finally granted me permission to tell his story. Yes, folks, by Week Three I have voices in my head. This is good (for the novel) and bad (for maintaining the pretence of sanity in front of family and friends). By now, I know these imaginary people better than I know my best friends.

But it's also easier to spot the ones that aren't working out, and there are always several. They seemed great at the start, but for some reason they failed to thrive. So I give them a mission (usually involving shouting, armed robbery, running away from home, discovering something that will change the world as we know it, bankruptcy, murder) and see if they come to life properly after that.

Meanwhile, my real characters stand around commenting on the action, tapping their feet impatiently and muttering about me getting back to their stories. If the faltering characters still don't shine, I can bump them off in some hideously descriptive way, leaving the rest reeling with shock and dealing with the aftermath. By the time I've done all that, I'm another 15k words up and heading for the bliss of Week Four.

ELIZABETH'S NANOWRIMO NOVELS INCLUDE *INTO THE DARKEST CORNER, REVENGE OF THE TIDE, HUMAN REMAINS, UNDER A SILENT MOON,* AND *BACK FROM THE RED.*

WHAT DO I DO IF I HIT 50,000 WORDS EARLY?

Every year, about 2 percent of National Novel Writing Month participants have that rare combination of fleet-fingered typing skills and well-oiled imaginations that allow them to hit 50,000 words after a couple of weeks.

If you find yourself among this golden group and cross the 50,000-word threshold in Week Three, write like the wind until you reach the end of the story. If you've typed "The End" and still have a couple of days (and some energy) remaining, dive back into the middle sections of your book and begin fleshing out and realigning text to fit with whatever changes in story direction you've enacted over the course of the novel. If that sounds too tiring, consider adding an epilogue detailing all of your characters' post-story exploits. Or a random prologue starring a llama! Or a handsome table of contents. Every reader loves a nice table of contents.

Week Three Exercises →

Putting Your Story on the Map

One of the worst things about being an adult is not getting to color as often as we should. This week, give your monitor-burned eyeballs a rest for an hour or so and go old-school, forsaking the computer for a big piece of blank paper and some colored pencils or crayons.

The goal of this exercise is to make a map of your fictional world. On the map, you should include all of your characters' homes, their schools or workplaces, and any places they've visited in the book. This may be the first time you've thought about the spatial layout of your world, so feel free to make things up as you go.

After you've placed everything that already exists in your book on the map, go in with a loose hand and start creatively filling in and adding other details and landmarks, everything from beaches to parks to clock towers to cathedrals to bondage-gear shops. It's okay to get a little crazy, adding an ancient amphitheater behind a dry cleaning shop, or a whale-harpooning station atop City Hall. The map is partially for referencing later, but it's also a creative exercise in its own right. It's a chance to draw up your world just for fun and to see if any of these off-the-cuff imaginings might be something you'd like to incorporate into your noveling reality.

Also, don't feel constrained to drawing just one kind of map. For dramas that unfold mostly indoors, you may want to create a floor-by-floor schematic drawing of the important homes, shops, or restaurants, rather than mapping your book on a street-by-street level. Topographic maps may be helpful if you're writing a story that relies on encampments or precipitous shifts in altitude.

Finally, make sure to color everything in as vividly as possible. Since this exercise is a great way to procrastinate from writing your book, take as long as you like perfecting the algae slick on the town pond with a realistic shade of green.

When you're done, keep the map close at hand as an updatable inspiration-generator and a handy reminder of where things are in your book.

The Person & Thing Game

For those looking to spice up their writing with some random (and word-count-bolstering) creativity, this exercise is a time-tested winner.

To play it, you'll need a public space and an unread newspaper. You'll also need a pen and your notebook. This works best as a two-player game, but it can also be fun as a solo challenge.

Here's how the game works: Sit in a public space with plenty of foot traffic. Close your eyes, and count to fifteen. When you open your eyes, the first person you see is your Person. Write down everything you can about your character before he or she gets away—clothes, carriage, race, hairstyle, what he or she's holding—anything and everything.

Next, take your newspaper and close your eyes again. Open your newspaper to a random page and, keeping your eyes closed, run your finger over the page, stopping after a couple of seconds.

The article, advertisement, or photo you're pointing to has a deep connection to the Person you just collected. What's the connection? You have to figure it out, and you have to work that person and their issue convincingly into the next chapter of your novel.

The more people you collect and successfully incorporate into each chapter, the more points you get in the game. If you're playing with someone else, you alternate collecting people and their issues; each person harvests his or her own random characters and looks up their backstories in the newspaper. Then both of you set off to write, coming back together at the end of the noveling period to read each other the passages featuring your random cameos.

WEEK THREE RECAP

REPUTATION:
→ A second wind cometh.

GOALS:
→ Hit the magical 35,000 point by the end of this week.
→ Power through the urges to quit.

DO:
→ Get out of the 20,000s quickly—they're literary quicksand.
→ Experiment with new writing locations.
→ Attempt at least one 6,000-word day.
→ Give minor characters a mission.
→ Map your world.
→ Begin truncating chapters as needed to nab a full story arc by month's end.

DON'T:
→ Quit. The best is just around the corner, and your story is about to start gelling in surprising ways.

REMEMBER:
→ The difference between a hopeless book and a (relatively) happy one is usually just a few hours of writing. The more you write, the more inspired you'll feel, and the easier each writing session will become.

⟩ TIPS FROM THE TRENCHES:
⟩ NANOWRIMO WINNERS ON WEEK THREE

What It Feels Like

"Week Three is like coming out of the desert to see a city in front of you. You're not at the city gates yet, but you're almost there. Just keep going."
—**PATRICIA PINTO,** SIX-TIME NANOWRIMO WINNER FROM PETALING JAYA, MALAYSIA

"The most annoying thing for me is the sudden realization that I'm halfway through my word count, but only a third of the way through my plot. I have to speed things up and adjust what happens when. Otherwise I'll have a terrible case of Everything Ends Suddenly in the Last Five Pages."
—**MARA JOHNSTONE,** TEN-TIME NANOWRIMO WINNER FROM SANTA ROSA, CALIFORNIA

"The flip-flopping! One day you're up (yay! in a groove here! so many words!), the next day you're really, really down (it's all still really shitty nonsense). The first few years I thought that was just me, but I now know it's part of the process."
—**MARRIJE SCHAAKE,** NINE-TIME NANOWRIMO WINNER FROM UTRECHT, THE NETHERLANDS

"The best part of the middle stretch is realizing that you do have enough ideas to write an entire novel."
—**MICHELLE BRECKON,** FIVE-TIME NANOWRIMO WINNER FROM STOW, OHIO

"At midmonth your real world and fantasy world will collide. Stay with the fantasy world."
—**REGINA KAMMER,** SEVEN-TIME NANOWRIMO WINNER FROM OAKLAND, CALIFORNIA

How to Rock It

"Trust the process—and yourself. It's okay to flounder and have no idea what you are doing. Just put one word after another and interesting, unexpected ideas are sure to surface."
—**EMILY BRISTOW,** ELEVEN-TIME NANOWRIMO WINNER FROM AUSTIN, TEXAS

"If it's November and you haven't been to a local NaNoWriMo get-together yet, it's time to find one. Week Three is where support of other writers helps so much. If you can't make it out, hit the NaNoWriMo forums . . . there are tens of thousands of other writers waiting to help you."

—HEATHER DUDLEY, SIX-TIME NANOWRIMO WINNER FROM MACON, GEORGIA

"Add more conflict!"

—SYAHIRA SHARIF, THREE-TIME NANOWRIMO WINNER FROM PETALING JAYA, MALAYSIA

"In Week Three I usually get my characters drunk. It's fun to write, I learn more how my characters operate with lower inhibitions, and it's a great excuse for all the typos."

—KAREN WILLSHER, EIGHT-TIME NANOWRIMO WINNER FROM EDMONTON, CANADA

"If you introduced a character or plot element in the beginning that hasn't been mentioned since, the middle stretch is a great time to bring it up again."

—SUJIN HEADRICK, ELEVEN-TIME NANOWRIMO WINNER FROM ATLANTA, GEORGIA

"Take time to celebrate hitting the halfway mark. If you're struggling, don't hide it. Having someone say, 'You can do it!' helps more than you might realize."

—ASHLEY MARTIN, FOUR-TIME NANOWRIMO WINNER FROM HELENA, MONTANA

"Don't think about word targets or the number of days left on the calendar. Just keep putting words into sentences."

—EMILY HOGARTH, FIVE-TIME NANOWRIMO WINNER FROM WELLS, UNITED KINGDOM

"I've been told many times that the point you want to quit anything is 75 percent. Don't be a statistic."

—SYDNEY HOFFA, TWO-TIME NANOWRIMO WINNER FROM OHIO ·

"The worst thing about the middle of NaNoWriMo is story fatigue. I recommend a refreshing beverage of your choice, and the immediate employment of whatever plot device would keep you interested if you were a reader, not the writer."

—KAIN FORAN, FIVE-TIME NANOWRIMO WINNER FROM MELBOURNE, AUSTRALIA

8. WEEK FOUR: CHAMPAGNE AND THE ROAR OF THE CROWD

Dear Writer,

This is where it all comes together. Week Four. The sink or swim, do or die, zero hour. Or hours. You have 168 of them left. Assuming you sleep eight hours a night, and are otherwise occupied twelve hours per day, that's 16 hours—or 1,680 plump, succulent word-filled writing minutes—ahead of you.

But before we delve too deeply into the math of your imminent triumph, I need you to do me a favor. I'd like you to put this book down, put on your shoes, grab your keys, and go to the grocery store.

Seriously.

Go now.

Okay, go later. Whenever it's convenient. But make sure, when you're at the store, to pick up two bottles of champagne. If you are underage, you can pick up a champagne substitute, such as beer.

Then bring the two bottles home and hide both away at the back of the fridge. We'll be needing them later.

Now, back to life in your novel.

It's Week Four. You're so close to the end of the month you can taste it. And whether you're at 14,000 or 40,000 words, there's probably a part of you that's asking: Haven't I written enough already? Do I *really* need to go any further? Why don't I just bow out now, and wrap up the manuscript in a couple of months, when I'm less tired and have a better supply of clean underwear?

These are all good questions.

And here's the answer: The next seven days will pass in the blink of an eye. To be replaced by another seven. And another seven after that.

Before you know it, the weeks will become months, which will fast become years. In no time, you'll be eighty-five years old and sitting on a porch somewhere, looking back on your life, and reminiscing about all the many things you've accomplished.

And when you get to that point, I promise you this: Those activities and errands that seem so essential right now—composing the company's annual report, passing that English exam, arranging for competent child care—all of these things that seem so crucial will not be recalled with pride or fondness.

In fact, you won't remember a single one of them.

Decades from now, however, you *will* remember that ineffable moment when the word counter ran its computery calculation over your book and announced you had reached the 50,000-word endpoint. You'll smilingly recall that time you were stupid enough to sign up for the challenge of a lifetime, and mighty enough to see it through. You will remember that month, that hectic, harried month, when you made a promise to yourself, when you set off on an impossible quixotic quest, and *nailed* it.

Do you see where I'm going with this?

You are on the verge of pulling off something incredible here. You have many more words to write and, given the short time remaining, success may involve hard work. But over these past three weeks you've honed all the skills you need to pull this off—to glide over that finish line.

You *can* do this. Just make the time to write, however much time it takes. Move forward, relentless, determined, confident.

And as you cross these last few miles, savor them. For the pain is almost over, and the celebrations are about to begin.

Week Four Issues ➔

Arriving at 35,000 Words

The only thing remotely close to the emotional elation of hitting 50,000 words is reaching 35,000 words. Everything eases up at 35,000. This is the penultimate lap; the on-ramp to the forties; the place where the chunk of work separating you from "The End" can be whittled down to nothing in a matter of days. Thirty-five thousand words is where you get your third wind, and the writing from here on out will remind you of those breezy, blissful days of Week One.

Holiday Horror Stories: Surviving Family Vacations with Your Word Count Intact

If you are writing your book during November or, God help you, December, you'll have the wildcard of the holidays thrown into your final writing sessions. Though these often mean time off work or school, they also bring a host of family obligations. Surviving Thanksgiving or Christmas with your word count intact takes some finessing, especially if it involves long drives and airport layovers.

If you are going to be ending your month with your family, the most important step is to let them know ahead of time that you'll be bringing a time-sucking project home with you. Explaining to your relatives that you'll be physically present for the holidays but not entirely mentally there can be accomplished tactfully by (re)using some of the "I'm writing a novel" talking points from Chapter 2.

Another time-tested holiday tip for endgame novelists is to rent a motel room instead of staying at a relative's house. This way, you'll always have a quiet, controlled writing retreat when you need it. If a motel is out of the question, or if you are hosting the holidays at your place, figure out in advance what room (or, more likely, what spidery corner of the basement) might be designated a semiprivate "writing area."

Twelve-time winner Erin Allday and her sister, Liana, found an extra bedroom served as a usable-if-imperfect writing station when their family came for a Thanksgiving visit one year.

"For four days, my parents and grandmother were staying with us in our two-bedroom apartment," Erin remembers. "My sister and I shared a bed and a computer for those four days. We regularly fought over who got to lock herself in the bedroom and write while the other one cooked and entertained.

"My parents, meanwhile, were not at all understanding about the importance of finishing our novels. We kept trying to explain why we had to retreat to the bedroom to write, but I think they assumed we were just trying to get away from all of the family."

If you know that working on your novel over the holiday is going to cause a family uprising, the best approach may be to lie. Explain that you are doing a family history project that requires you to shut yourself away from the family for most of the holiday so you can better recollect some of the memorable things Grandma has said at the dinner table over the years.

Crossing the Finish Line

Yep. It's going to happen this week. I tend to celebrate crossing over with a meditative ceremony where I print the book out and neatly stack its pages on the floor. When everything has been properly laid out, I take a few steps back from the work, close my eyes, and offer up my thanks to the writing powers for another bountiful harvest. At which point, I get a running start and dive headlong into my word-pile, rolling around and snorting like a pig.

And then I fall asleep for three days.

How you celebrate is up to you. But know you can't possibly overdo the whooping, hollering, and carrying on. No matter what your neighbors might say.

Week Four Tips →

Love Your Body

After three weeks of high-intensity typing, even the most robust bodies are feeling some pain. From your wrists to your hands to your back and neck, the human body wasn't made to do the kind of gloriously sustained creative work that you've spent the last three weeks putting it through. Throughout this final week, you should pay special attention to your body's needs, and take breaks every fifteen minutes to stretch the muscles in your shoulders and arms. During Week Four, your eyes will also take on the feel of desiccated cashews. Don't rub them: What they need is for you to stop staring so intently at your screen monitor for hours on end. Make a point of looking back and forth, from the far distance to the near distance, every five minutes or so.

Troll Your Novel Notes File for Forgotten Ideas

In the manic pace of the last week, you may completely forget that genius plot turn you came up with in the previous weeks. As Week Four begins, look through both your noveling notebook and your computer novel notes file to make sure you get in all the good stuff before the curtain closes on the month.

Cross Early and Keep Writing

As I've mentioned, you are currently enveloped by a special badass writing energy that will dissipate when the four weeks expire. If you

EMBRACE THE CRAZY

BY MARISSA MEYER

It's Week Four, and whether you're sitting pretty at 45k, or preparing yourself for one mad, miraculous sprint to the end, one thing is inevitable during this week: You're about to experience a serious case of novel-induced insanity.

We all start to feel a little loopy by Week Four. You'll recognize the symptoms of novel-induced insanity when you start giggling hysterically during the tragic death scene of your hero's beloved sidekick. Or when it suddenly seems like a good idea to drop an invasion of roller-skating penguins into your quiet historical romance. Or when you start posting absurd, out-of-context teaser sentences on Facebook and then rant angrily to your cat when none of your friends "Like" them.

Once you've diagnosed yourself with this affliction, don't fight it. Embrace it. Allow yourself to enjoy the madness and euphoria that comes with writing a novel in thirty days. After all, you're a *novelist,* and we novelists have to uphold our longstanding reputation as a crazy bunch. So build yourself a secret writing fort out of sofa cushions where you can safely plot out that last climactic battle scene. Don a feather boa or pirate's hat while you swoon your way through that epic confession of love. Go outside and shake your fist at the heavens and proclaim that you are a fierce warrior of the written word, a conqueror of subplots and misbehaving characters!

Because this week, as you race toward that 50,000-word mark, it's important to remember that while writing can be tough and exhausting, it can also be a whole lot of fun.

MARISSA'S NANOWRIMO NOVELS INCLUDE *CINDER, SCARLET, CRESS,* AND *HEARTLESS.*

still have a couple of days left to go in the month after you cross the 50k finish line, try to get back in the writing saddle after your celebration and keep going. Everything you can do now will pay off huge dividends later. Plus, building up a wordy surplus before the month draws to a close means you can go back and delete all those abysmal italicized passages and still have a 50,000-word novel to show your friends at the month's close.

When It Happens, Tell Everyone You Know

It's clear that the satisfaction of having written a book in a month is its own reward for this crazy endeavor. A better reward, however, is bragging to all your friends and loved ones about your enormous accomplishment. And the best way to maximize your boasting potential is by sharing a screen shot of your winning word count on social media.

Here's one way to do it on a PC:

- ☑ Take your novel to a page that you won't mind your family and friends reading (the title page is a classy option).
- ☑ Go up and select Word Count for the entire novel, and make sure the square word count box displaying the total is visible in the middle of the screen.
- ☑ Find the Print Screen button on your keyboard. Note: It may be deviously labeled "Prt Scrn." When you hit the button, it will take a picture of whatever is on your screen at the time.
- ☑ Go to Programs, then Accessories, and open the cheap-o default paint program that came with your computer (it will probably be called Paint).
- ☑ Go up to the Edit drop-down menu and select the Paste option.
- ☑ You should now see the photo of your word-processing screen that your computer took a few seconds earlier.
- ☑ Save the file somewhere on your desktop, and then post it all over your social media outlets of choice.

Mac users activate their screen capture by hitting the command, shift, and "3" keys simultaneously. This will save a file (probably

THE (COLD) WINDS OF CHANGE: PUTTING WEATHER IN YOUR STORY

> "Nothing breaks up an author's progress like having to stop every few pages to fuss-up the weather."
>
> **—MARK TWAIN**

Weather is one of those things you don't really think about while you're reading a novel. Unlike the weather in real life, novel weather is mostly a low-key affair. Either it's cold or hot, rainy or not. If you find yourself winding your story down before you hit 50,000 words, consider spending some time adding exquisite weather to your book. Describe the warm winds and put smells in the air. Send in a monsoon, and follow a raindrop in its broken progress from cloud to gutter. Weather, as boring as it sounds, can actually be amazingly fun to write.

called "Photo One") to your startup disk, which can then be opened and cropped in a paint or design program.

Week Four Exercises →

Doing the Last Days Longhand: Your Novel, Unplugged

If you're far behind schedule, ignore this exercise completely and continue your typing frenzy. If you've managed to build up a word cushion, though, consider unplugging yourself from your computer this week and walking across the finish line *au naturel*.

That's right, I'm talking about the lost art of longhand noveling. By writing part of your book with pen and paper, you'll be forced to take your story slower (something you probably haven't been doing much of this month), giving you the chance to reflect a little before committing words to the page. There's something sensual and calming about writing by hand, and if there's something we all could use a little more of in Week Four, it's calm.

For advice on taking a longhand vacation, I asked one-time winner Jennifer McCreedy, one of only a half dozen or so NaNoWriMo participants to have written their 50,000-word novels entirely by hand, to give us her top four tips:

- ☑ Buy a notebook with lined paper that does not have perforated sheets. Opt for notebooks with a more durable binding than your average glue—look for ones with sewn bindings.
- ☑ Give yourself, and your tired writing hand, a break. If you start to run low on ideas, stop writing and let your mind and hands recharge at the same time. If you're having a burst of inspiration that's driving you to write for hours, force yourself to take breaks when you come to the end of a chapter or the top of the hour.
- ☑ Don't worry about adding each line to your word count as you write it. Instead, count when you stop for the day, or when you pause to give your writing hand a break. Write your updated word count at the top of your last written page, so that you can easily locate it when you tally up your next section.

HOW TO MAKE YOUR PRINTOUT LOOK MORE LIKE A REAL BOOK

For a truly polished presentation, number your pages and your chapters, and insert a page break after the end of each chapter. Now change the document layout to the Landscape setting, and then divide each page into two very wide columns with a two-inch gutter between them. Voilà! Bookish, indeed.

☑ Don't buy expensive pens to novel with. Ten thousand words later, your pen will start to run out of ink, and you'll be $7 in the hole. Go for a pack of inexpensive (but not dollar-store) pens with blue or black permanent ink. Avoid erasable ink, as you'll be tempted to make edits—even if you have a will of iron. For the same reasons, don't novel longhand in pencil.

Reintroducing Yourself to the World as a Novelist

One fringe benefit of writing a book is being seen by those around you in the new, vastly sexier light of your novelist status. Displaying your new writer self may feel uncomfortable at first, but give it a try. Social gatherings are a great place to practice the brilliant self-absorption that you'll need to emanate as a novelist.

Maximizing the benefits of a party situation is a learned skill, and it can be difficult for novice writers, especially as the party wears on and the patrons become increasingly drunk and prone to talking about all manner of things, most of which are unrelated to your novel.

Steering every conversation back to your book isn't impossible, though. It just requires a certain amount of conversational finesse. Witness the following model tête-à-tête:

> **Writer:** So, what's up, partygoer?
>
> **Partygoer:** Not much! I've been pretty sick lately with that flu that's been going around, so I've just been laying low. Sleeping a lot. You know ...
>
> **Writer:** Oh, man! That's so funny you would say that. The protagonist in my novel had this moment where he thought about opening an office supply store that sold only wiener dogs.
>
> **Partygoer (laughing):** What a brilliant plot idea! I feel better already!
>
> **Writer:** Yeah. Cracked me up, too. But he didn't end up doing it. Maybe in the sequel, huh?
>
> **Partygoer (getting out a pen):** I need your autograph right now.

Another key point to remember—whether developing your sterling literary reputation at social gatherings or one-on-one—is that the novel you just completed is *not* your first novel. Even if it is, in fact, your first novel. In all conversations, you should refer to your manuscript as "my most recent novel."

Technically speaking, this is accurate. And it also implies the existence of a host of other, earlier novels whose existence you are humble enough not to get into at that moment. In the unlikely situation that someone asks for a synopsis of your earlier novels, say your agent has asked you not to talk about them. Then roll your eyes, shrug your shoulders, and sigh, "The *publishing* world . . ."

WEEK FOUR RECAP

REPUTATION:
→ The glorious sprint home.

GOALS:
→ Explore out prologues, epilogues, and alternate endings if you run out of story before you hit 50k.
→ Sketch out the final chapters if you're running out of time.
→ Call in favors to have as much noveling time as possible in the home stretch.
→ Ice the champagne.

DO:
→ Make big change happen in your story.
→ Get your characters out of their comfort zones and take away the things they need most.
→ Let your cheerleaders contribute story ideas.
→ Write every day (even if you're only writing a few words).
→ Embrace ridiculous word-count padding tricks if your story has stalled.

DON'T:
→ Feel despondent if your writing buddies are ahead of you! You're almost done!

REMEMBER:
→ Come-from-behind victories are a time-honored part of NaNoWriMo—some writers do the whole 50k in the last week. Wherever you are now, you can get to 50k!

TIPS FROM THE TRENCHES:
NANOWRIMO WINNERS ON WEEK FOUR

What It Feels Like

"The last day is like the last mile of a marathon—you're about to puke, your legs are wobbly, and sometimes even death seems preferable—but you've come so far and the end is on the horizon. That final push can be mind-numbing, but it's totally worth it every time."
—ANGELA LINDFORS, FIVE-TIME NANOWRIMO WINNER FROM SAN ANTONIO, TEXAS

"In the last couple days of NaNoWriMo, I get my plot rolling. And I cry and beg November to be longer because now I finally have a story."
—AMY ROHOZEN, THREE-TIME NANOWRIMO WINNER FROM CLEVELAND, OHIO

"I find that my hands can ache during the last week from so much typing. In that case, I do small bursts such as 500-word sprints and then give my hands massages while I decide what I'm going to write next."
—KAIN FORAN, FIVE-TIME NANOWRIMO WINNER FROM MELBOURNE, AUSTRALIA

"Finishing is bittersweet. It's like saying good-bye to an old friend, albeit a best friend who's been living with you rent-free and eating all your food. So you don't necessarily want them living with you anymore, but when they're gone, you miss all the great conversations and crazy late-night parties."
—ELIA WINTERS, TWELVE-TIME NANOWRIMO WINNER FROM NORTHAMPTON, MASSACHUSETTS

"My favorite part is looking back at the novel that you meant to write and comparing it to the mostly finished novel that you have in your hands. I love throwing in a little tribute to the novel I had originally planned on writing, whether that's a cameo appearance of the original protagonist before the comedic relief character stepped in and took control, or a reference to the time-traveling plot I scrapped on Day One."
—BETH CARTER, NINE-TIME NANOWRIMO WINNER FROM WASHINGTON, DC

How to Rock It

"Write the ending, regardless of how far away you think you are."
—ROYCE ROESWOOD, FOUR-TIME NANOWRIMO WINNER FROM DENVER, COLORADO

"Don't listen to that voice inside your head that says 38,000 words is fine."
—DARLENE REILLEY, SIX-TIME NANOWRIMO WINNER FROM SPANAWAY, WASHINGTON

"Don't worry if it's not feeling nearly as complete or as mind-blowing as you hoped. You're still bound for glory. You may have to pull an all-nighter to hit the deadline, but it's just that one night. And it feels kinda rock 'n' roll."
—JANE ORMOND, THREE-TIME NANOWRIMO WINNER FROM MELBOURNE, AUSTRALIA

"In the past, I have had to make up 10k–15k words in the last week of NaNo to meet my word-count goal. If this is you, I would consider taking a personal day from work and hammering out the last bit. It made me much more productive when I went back to work."
—MADELINE TURNIPSEED, TWO-TIME NANOWRIMO WINNER FROM BRYAN, TEXAS

"If I'm down to the wire and I have a great deal more to write, I will often spend the last few days of the month writing a detailed synopsis for the rest of the book."
—MICHAEL SIROIS, TEN-TIME NANOWRIMO WINNER FROM SPRING, TEXAS

"Limit input. No reading until you hit your word count for the day, no TV, no movies."
—ALI HAWKE, EIGHT-TIME NANOWRIMO WINNER FROM ST. LOUIS, MISSOURI

"Always remember that there are people who have completed the 50,000 words in under a day. No matter how far behind you think you are, there is always time to catch up."
—LIEKE BRAADBAART, FOUR-TIME NANOWRIMO WINNER FROM ABERDEEN, UNITED KINGDOM

"Skip ahead to the good bits, the ones that get your blood racing, make you laugh until you cry, or cause you to cringe in horror that such a gross scene came from inside your brain. You're not done until 11:59 p.m. on the 30th. You are a champion, not a quitter, and every word is another victory."
—KAREN WILLSHER, EIGHT-TIME NANOWRIMO WINNER FROM EDMONTON, CANADA

For you to read upon reaching 50,000 words
or the end of the month, whichever comes first.

Dear Novelist,

Congratulations! It is my pleasure to inform you that you have officially kicked ass this month.

No matter how many words you wrote, you did an amazing thing. Through distractions and demands and family obligations, you forged ahead. Your willingness to go out on a creative limb, to stand up and reach an impossible goal, is an inspiring example to all of us.

For those of you who managed to write 50,000 words this month, know that writing so much so quickly is a task that most professional writers would run from screaming. You have eaten the challenge for breakfast, and cleaned your teeth with its bones. You are brave, talented, and brimming with the kind of loquacious storytelling skills that will serve you well in your new job as up-and-coming novelist.

And if you fell a little short of 50,000 but still wrote your heart out, I have a little secret to share: In the course of this great experiment in caffeine

Consumption, the goal of 50,000 words has been, shall we say, overemphasized. One of the things month-long noveling does is get your sense of scale all out of whack. This is done intentionally, because anyone with a realistic sense of perspective wouldn't try to write a novel in a month.

As the month ends, though, I feel it is my ethical responsibility to bring some perspective back into your life. So please listen closely: If you "only" wrote 15,000 words over the past four weeks, you invented fifty (that's five-oh) book pages of fiction. Those of you who made it to the 25,000-word point wrote eighty-three pages! In a <u>month</u>. Hello?

This is something to write home about. And in this letter home, you should include a few things. One of them being the fact that you chose to <u>try</u>. This may seem like a little thing — this trying — but it is not. You put your name out there for the world to see. You risked failure. And just by risking failure, you avoided it entirely.

Let me explain. You could have spent this month living your normal life. You could have gone for long walks with your significant other or won points with your boss by coming into work without those big bags under your eyes. Instead, you agreed to do something dumb. You agreed to try and write more fiction in a month than most people do in a lifetime.

Many of you may not normally write fiction. Maybe you previously saw fiction as something other people write. But this month, you dared to say, "Screw that. It's my turn." You stepped up to the plate. And there's nothing more admirable in this whole world than someone willing to set for themselves the fearsome task of trying something big.

So be proud, writer. You've done a fantastic thing this month, and I salute you for it.

Now please do me a favor and go grab those bottles of champagne (or champagne substitute) you bought in Chapter 8. One of the bottles is for you. And the other is a gift for your MVPs: the friends and family who helped you through this tumultuous month.

And as you gather with your loved ones to celebrate, please accept my congratulations, and a thank you! on behalf of everyone who will eventually read and love your book. You've done a fantastic thing this month, writer, and I salute you for it.

Chris

9. I WROTE A NOVEL. NOW WHAT?

It's been a month of stress and jubilation, panic and triumph. And now, somehow, it's over.

After all the frenzied productivity and bursts of creative accomplishment, you'll likely find your return to normal life a little . . . weird. Truman Capote famously compared finishing a book to taking a favorite child outside and shooting him. While your book is still a few steps away from being finished, you *have* completed a huge portion of it, and you will be feeling the tingles of loss, emptiness, and powder burn that Capote described in the coming weeks.

NaNoWriMo participants refer to this feeling of aimlessness as the "post-NaNo Blues" or "post-novel depression." Whatever it's called, I've come down with a case of it each of the fourteen years I've written a novel. At the close of Week Four, I feel like I'm being wrenched awake from a beautiful dream. I don't know what to do with myself, and all I want to do is go see what my characters are up to.

But as soon as the deadline lifts, my connection to that fantasy world flickers, and the real world comes rushing back. As you come down off your writer's high this week, you too will be deluged with an array of chores and errands; the everyday must-dos that you've been so rightly putting off for the past month to focus on your writing.

Your immediate instinct when faced with such a bewildering array of stimulus may be to burrow back into the comfortably snug confines of your fictional world.

Don't do it.

Despite what you may have learned last month, sustained writing is best accomplished as part of a balanced lifestyle, one that includes things like grocery shopping and speaking in complete sentences with your significant other. No matter how dreadful it seems, you should take a vacation from your novel, for at least a couple of weeks, to get some perspective on what you just wrote.

Trust me: The novel is going to be right there waiting for you when you get back. Right now, your friends, family, and creditors are calling. Spend the coming month getting reacquainted with the distractions that you successfully avoided during the last one.

And when all of that is done; when calm has been attained; when you've gotten a little distance from your manuscript, *then* you will be ready for the next awesome experience: reading it.

Turning the Pages and Making the Call →

After some well-deserved R&R, heed Julia Crouch's Guest Pep Talk and make a date with your novel. When you've finished reading it, ask yourself the following question: Do I want to devote a year or more of my life to making it better?

The answer may be no. And that's an okay answer. *No Plot? No Problem!* is as much a guide to recharging your imagination as it is a path toward book production. With our busy lives, we have to pick our battles, and there's every chance that you just won't like the book you wrote enough to wrangle it into shape.

Five of the fourteen novels I've written fit into this category. The first time it happened, I was devastated. It was my second NaNoWriMo, and I made the mistake I describe in Chapter 2, one common among second-year participants: I got overly ambitious with my characters, and I allowed all sorts of depressing nonsense from my Magna Carta II list to sneak in.

The next year, I thought I had learned my lesson, but once again I waded knee-deep into the trough of failure. This time I kept the characters on such a tight rein that the book ended up feeling claustrophobic and overwritten, plagued with a lack of action and a jaw-dropping amount of filler.

With back-to-back noveling failures to my credit, "exuberant imperfection" started seeming less like a panic-free way to get monumental tasks accomplished and more like a surefire way to make me feel like a moron. Not caring if I wrote crap and stumbling into passable prose was exhilarating. Not caring if I wrote crap and getting exactly that for two years in a row was demoralizing.

Just as I was about to drop my laptop into a trash compactor, though, a friend of mine sent me some quotes from the celebrated graphic designer Bruce Mau. One of which struck pretty close to home.

"Love your experiments (as you would an ugly child)," Mau's maxim went. "Exploit the liberty in casting your work as beautiful experiments, iterations, attempts, trials, and errors. Take the long view and allow yourself the fun of failure every day."

As corny as it sounds, those words changed the way I looked at my two crapulent works of fiction. As literature, they were ugly as sin. As experiments, though, they were packed with a useful array of wrong turns, misguided decisions, and shameful flops. From those experiments, I discovered copious amounts about what I shouldn't be writing. This allowed me to spend my subsequent novels in the happy pursuit of what I should.

Inspiration and insight, I've learned, flow more freely from failures than they do from successes. Even if your novel is beyond editorial salvation, your imagination has gotten a great workout, and you'll likely have a much easier time on whatever creative challenge you tackle next.

And if your answer is yes, you would like to revise your manuscript to perfection—well, roll up those sleeves and read on.

Whittling the Stump: The Knotty Issues of Rewriting →

Rewriting is when your novel—the version that people will fight one another for in bookstores—is born. What you spent the last thirty days creating amounts to a large, knotty wooden stump. It's a powerful, brute object, and it's absolutely amazing that you conjured such a dense mass out of thin air. But it's also likely too unwieldy at this point to take outside the home.

In the editing process, that stump will get whittled into a lithe instrument that will eventually leave literary agents clutching their hearts in fear and wonder.

Making the myriad tweaks, fixes, and alterations necessary to get your book reader-ready is a huge, challenging project. When you realize that most novels on the bookstore shelf were not rewritten once but five, six, or ten times, you will begin to see why even the youngest professional novelists have the skittish,

HOW LONG DOES A REWRITE USUALLY TAKE?

Rewrites vary, of course, but a year is a pretty good estimate for completing a second draft. If you're focused and spend every weekend revising, you may be able to do it in half that.

EMERGING FROM THE NANO TUNNEL

BY JULIA CROUCH

So it has all ground to a halt. Like a spinning plate, your novel has come to rest (and possibly fallen off the pole). Life seems emptier than before, now you don't have that daily word-count engine to keep you going. But never fear! You now have three tasks ahead of you.

The first sounds easy, but it's probably the hardest: Do not show your novel to anyone.

As you surface from your NaNo tunnel, you may well think you have produced the next *Anna Karenina*. But remember, your inner critics are still sunning their legs on holiday. Do yourself, your novel, and the friend you thought might like it a favour. Do not show!

The second is more fun: Detox.

You have to get the rest of your life back into shape. Allow yourself to leave the words behind and reacquaint yourself with fresh air, friends, children, and partners. Actually cook some real food. Perhaps get a little exercise. Because you are going to have to be in tiptop condition for your third task: Make a date with your novel.

If it's a November novel, you could reserve New Year's Day—the birthplace of all good intentions—for this. Ninety-five per cent of the time you will cringe. You will read from behind your fingers, you will gasp "NO!" and you will feel either like running away or going to sleep to escape the horror. However, for the remaining 5 per cent of your read-through, you might find yourself smiling, nodding, possibly even going "*Oh,* yeah."

These are healthy ratios. Remember this. Don't expect too much. And, if you think it's got even a smidgeon of potential, well then, what's the rush? You've got the rest of your life to lick it into shape.

JULIA'S NANOWRIMO NOVELS INCLUDE *CUCKOO*, *EVERY VOW YOU BREAK*, AND *TARNISHED*.

prematurely aged appearance of people who have endured a lifetime of unspeakable tragedies.

The good news, though, is that the difficulties of rewriting are absolutely worth it, and that taking your novel from the rough draft stage to the shining, breathtaking end product will delight and devastate you just as intensely as the rough draft did, if not more so.

Trading Chain Saws for Dental Picks (and the Return of a Familiar Secret Weapon) →

In my experience, the basic key to editing is this: Slow down. This is especially true for those of us who spent a month writing our rough drafts at literary Warp Factor Ninety. If you attack your second draft with the same reckless zeal that you used to such triumphant effect on your first draft, you'll end up hurtling right past almost all of the fine-tunings that your second draft needs.

This reduced pace will feel excruciating at first, especially because you know you have so much ground to cover. But it's simply painstaking, brow-furrowing work, meant to be taken one page at a time. The days of the chain saw are over; from here on out, we'll be using dental picks.

Oh, and a secret weapon.

Unlike the devilish device you met in Chapter 1—the deadline—this writing aid is actually an old acquaintance of yours. One we've been keeping locked up in our kennels for the past month.

Yes, your Inner Editor is ready to come home.

I know, I know: This is not the greatest news. You've been doing just fine without all the nit-picking, second-guessing, and perfectionist carping that you've come to expect from your Inner Editor.

However, only your Inner Editor can help you spot all the improvements your novel needs. And besides, your Inner Editor's stay in the kennel has done it a world of good. It's mellowed and tanned; it's become, dare I say it, a kinder, gentler Inner Editor. Frankly, I think the fact that you've done such fantastic work without its help has humbled it a little bit.

So the caustic, biting days are over. From here on out, the criticism will be (mostly) constructive, and I think you two would make an excellent team on this upcoming project.

So are you ready to have it back?

 ← PRESS HERE

Just touch the button, and it's yours.

Now let's dive into that rewrite.

The Big Picture: Entering the War Room →

There are a bunch of great ways to begin a novel revision. Some authors use spreadsheets to chart the emotional tenor of each scene. Others jot down their scenes on note cards (real or digital) and then shuffle and tweak the deck until they have a story arc they love. Author Lani Diane Rich's Guest Pep Talk on page 182 highlights a no-nonsense approach where she makes a list of her book's problems and then just starts in at Chapter 1 and fixes them one by one.

Me? I like to start by watching old World War II movies. Pretty much any one of them will do, as long as it contains that classic scene where anxious generals crowd around a map on a tabletop, where someone is pushing tiny brigades around with a shuffleboard stick.

CREATING A NOVEL BLOOPERS FILE

Just as one of the first things you did when you started writing was to create a "Novel Notes" file on your computer, so should you now create a "Novel Cuts" file. Use this as the home for every deletion longer than a couple of sentences. You might change your mind about that deleted scene later, and you'll also want to have the unexpurgated version of the book on hand when the biographers come sniffing around your estate in a couple of decades.

Why are these commanders playing with miniatures in a life-or-death moment? Because in perilous situations, getting a bird's-eye view helps you see the right way forward. Scale models allow you to play out various scenarios in a low-risk way, trying different approaches until you find one that works. When you're in the trenches of novel revision, surrounded by those dense thickets of words, it's easy to get off track, and start pushing forward in the wrong direction.

Which is why the first step I recommend in a novel-revision campaign is creating a miniature version of your book. I like to do this by writing a short synopsis of every chapter, describing the characters, the action, and the tone of the scene.

Here's an example of a chapter synopsis from a young adult novel I've been working on:

"Steven makes dinner for himself and waits for his sister, Billa, to come home. When she finally appears in the driveway, though, she's with an unexpected guest: the mega-popular Kevin Sturp. Steven, confused about why someone like Kevin would be hanging out with his weirdo sister (and embarrassed by the squalor of their house), hides in the bathroom. There, he overhears Kevin and his sister discussing something deeply disturbing they just discovered in the off-limits tunnels that run beneath their town."

Okay. Hemingway, it is not. And even looking at it now, I'm tempted to tweak the scene a little bit. But for now, the goal is just to summarize each chapter in your book as it currently stands. All you need at this point is to see the lay of the land; winning the battle will come next.

Go through and write up a synopsis for all of your chapters. When you're done, the arc of your story will be laid bare, a fact that will either be exciting or depressing, depending on how cohesive your book turned out. No matter how tight the tale, though, there is still plenty of room for improvement. Which is what we'll do now.

Focusing the Story

As you look over the story, you'll likely spot one or two (or ten) digressions. While writing your first draft, these tangents were vibrant labs for the production of new ideas and angles. And let's face it: They were also easy ways to amass the day's word-count quota.

There's no shame in that. Now, though, you need to decide what really belongs in your book. Go ahead and cut the obvious filler scenes, archiving all of them into a separate Word doc in case you decide to bring them back later.

Now, look at your cast of characters. Does it include more people than your book really needs? Some of those superfluous voices may be evolutionary vestiges of earlier, discarded story directions. If there are any you can do without, cut them now. In your character audit, you may find an underused but lovable stowaway who you're reluctant to evict. Think about crafting a new relationship or twist that might bind the person more tightly to the core of your story. As you come up with new story and character ideas, add them to the synopsis!

Once you've finalized your cast, consider whether everyone is developed enough. Do all of your characters get the screen time they need? This is especially important if you've written the story from the viewpoints of several different people.

As you ponder your characters, think about the through-lines of each character. One classic storytelling technique is to establish in the first chapter what each character wants more than anything else in the world, along with the fears or obstacles that prevent them from getting it. The plot is your protagonist's quest for that precious thing, and their character arc becomes the ways in which they are transformed by the journey. Your supporting characters (and villain, if you have one!) will also have their own quests and needs. By the end of the tale, everyone may not have gotten *exactly* what they wanted, but they all will have changed in some interesting ways.

Fixing the Flow

Which brings us to the next phase of the synopsis-eyeballing: tightening your book's pacing. After you've trimmed all the obvious fat and have the essential scenes blocked out, it's time to address questions of flow, tension, and payoff.

Here are some questions you might ask yourself as you rework the synopsis. Does it seem like the story gets off to a dynamic start at the beginning, only to lose steam in the middle? Do the opening chapters have too much exposition and not enough action? How might you shuffle scenes or use flashbacks to heighten the story's drama, comedy, or suspense?

This is the beauty of using a synopsis, since you can easily take the story apart and reassemble it in any number of ways. Give it a shot now, moving things around and making tweaks until you have a story that builds on itself in a way that feels engaging and right to you.

MAKING YOUR ROUGH DRAFT PRESENTABLE TO THE NEIGHBORS

BY LANI DIANE RICH

There's a statistic out there that over 90 percent of writers who start novels never finish them. You've come out on the sweeter-smelling side of that stat. Be proud—drafting a book is a hell of an accomplishment. But now you're staring down the barrel of the next stage: Revision. Here's my advice:

First, put the book away and don't think about it for a while. Six weeks usually does the trick, but the important thing is that you stay away long enough that the details get a little fuzzy for you. That gives you distance so that when you go back into your draft, you can see it through the eyes of the reader, which is what you need, because revision is all about making your wild, crazy, sex-haired rough draft into something presentable for the neighbors.

Second, when you go back to your book, just read and take notes of your impressions. You can do this with a physical printout using flags and Post-its—I've never met a writer who'd miss an opportunity to hit the office supply store—or, if you'd prefer, you can do it electronically using commenting and track changes in your word-processing program. Either way, make your comments from a reader's perspective.

Once you've got your notes organized, go back in, beginning to end, and fix it as you go. During this sweep, you fix the structural problems, the murky motivations, and you kill your darlings—the scenes that don't move the story forward must go. A hint: If you can lift it out of the book entirely and not break the story, you don't need it.

Last is your final pass; your spell check, your grammar check, your continuity. This is where you let the Type A part of your personality out to play, tucking in all the loose ends and making it look neat for your next phase: beta readers.

Congratulations on getting that draft done, and don't dread revision. It's way more fun than it seems!

LANI'S NANOWRIMO NOVELS INCLUDE *TIME OFF FOR GOOD BEHAVIOR, MAYBE BABY,* AND *WISH YOU WERE HERE.*

Getting a Second Opinion: Beta Readers

When your synopsis is done, I'd recommend sending it out to readers for feedback. It may seem early, but getting responses from folks you trust while you're still building the book's foundation will save you a lot of work down the line.

When thinking about who should be on your team of literary mechanics, be sure to prioritize readers who love the same stories you do. At this point, you want input from people who are well-versed in your book's genre.

I find that having three to five beta readers is ideal; other writers rely on one or two trusted advisers. Whatever the size of your reading pool, come up with a list of the things you'd like them to look for before you hand over the book (or, in this case, the synopsis). Should they be pointing out typos? Flagging unbelievable plot twists? Mentioning places where they get confused? Bored?

Find out if your readers would prefer a printed or digital copy, and when you hand it over, be sure to give them a deadline as well. For a synopsis, a week is plenty. For an entire novel, a month is good, and will give the overachievers in your group time to read it twice.

When the day comes for them to give you the verdict, try to do it live—either in person, via video chat, or on the phone—instead of over email. Start by asking them what they liked, and don't be afraid to draw out the kudos! Many beta readers (correctly) understand that their job is to help you spot problems, so they will often give short shrift to the wonderful parts. But praise is essential, and not just for the good of your ego. You need to understand what's already working, so you don't accidentally mess it up in the next draft.

As they get into the long list of ways the book can be improved, just listen, take notes, and stifle any impulse to argue, explain, or point out the places you already have the thing they claim the story lacks. If they didn't see it, other people are going to miss it too. Just thank them for their great input, hide your mounting sense of panic, and ask enough follow-up questions so you're completely clear on their critiques.

Then repeat the process with another reader. And another. If you have good readers, you should come out of these sessions feeling a little despondent. Just remember that every manuscript is fixable, and getting these tough notes early on will make your book irresistible by the time it lands on the *New York Times* reviewer's desk.

That said, be sure to wait until you've talked to all of your beta readers before deciding what changes to make, and always sit with the combined feedback for a week or two before embarking on the next draft. Sometimes a beta reader will suggest a tweak that, at first

FROM RANDOM TANGENT TO INTERNATIONAL BEST SELLER:
ERIN MORGENSTERN AND *THE NIGHT CIRCUS*

Erin Morgenstern's journey to best-sellerdom began during her third NaNoWriMo. Her novel was losing steam, and she thought a wild detour might liven the story up. So she sent her entire cast off to the circus.

She fell in love with the place her characters discovered—a mysterious, late-night realm where impossible feats of magic abounded. The next NaNoWriMo, Erin crafted a brand-new tale set at the same circus, and then spent the following November adding 50,000 words to the story.

She edited the book herself, then started sending query letters to agents.

"I was prepared to get rejections across the board," she says. But many of the agents wrote back immediately, eager to read her book. She took a deep breath and sent it off.

That was when the bad news started rolling in. "I had one agent send me a very nice email," Erin reports, "that basically said I hurt his brain."

The consensus from three interested agents was that the book had great atmosphere, but lacked a compelling story. The idea of tearing apart her beloved circus and creating new character arcs was so daunting that she tried a few small fixes instead. "I added stuff I *thought* was plot: I made things explode. I put in some time travel."

She sent the revised book back to those agents, who weren't impressed. "That was the point," she says, "when I realized that I needed to think about it in an entirely different way."

She put the project away for a few months, and wrote a different manuscript for NaNoWriMo. Then she returned, refreshed, to *The Night Circus* and spent five months rebuilding the book from the ground up. New characters. More conflict. And a love story.

This was the book the agents had been waiting for, and all three of them wanted to represent it. She signed with one, and did another revision based on his notes. After a bidding war, the book was purchased by Doubleday for a high six-figure advance. Since its debut, *The Night Circus* has sold more than a million copies and has been translated into thirty languages.

Erin's advice for folks editing their manuscripts? Embrace the fact that your book will change dramatically between the first and final drafts. "Revision is a much messier process than it seems from the outside," she says. "Be flexible, and know that it might take a lot of stages to get it right. And be nice to yourself. Chocolate helps a lot."

glance, seems to fix every problem in your book. If you spend a few days pondering that change's impact on the rest of the tale, though, it rarely turns out to be the panacea you'd hoped. Neil Gaiman has a great quote about feedback from beta readers: "When people tell you something's wrong or doesn't work for them, they are almost always right," he writes. "When they tell you exactly what they think is wrong and how to fix it, they are almost always wrong."

In my experience, beta readers are right about exactly what's wrong *and* how to fix it fairly often. But remember: This is your book, and following your vision for it is the most important thing, even if it conflicts with advice from your beta team. Write the story *you* want to read, and your future fans will thank you for it.

Now take your reader's feedback and do another quick pass on your synopsis. When that's done, dive into your second draft.

The Small Picture: Polishing Your Prose →

After a few drafts, it will be time to address the sentence-level changes that will make your prose sparkle. There are a few small-picture messes particular to month-long novels.

The first of these is wooden prose. As you read through your book, you may be a little surprised at the starkness of the language.

LITERARY AGENT ARIELLE ECKSTUT ON LANDING THE RIGHT AGENT FOR YOUR BOOK

So you're done with your rewrite and ready to land an agent. Great! I asked Arielle Eckstut, an agent-at-large for the Levine Greenberg Literary Agency, cofounder of The Book Doctors, and coauthor with David Henry Sterry of *The Essential Guide to Getting Your Book Published*, to offer her advice on sending your book out into the agent-o-sphere. Here's what she had to say:

"RULE 1: Don't send a rough draft. Before you send your manuscript to an agent, make sure you've done everything you possibly can to make it the very best it can be. In fact, it's ideal to have a number of people read and comment on your manuscript before you send it off because there's simply no way to have the kind of objectivity you need on your own. The best kinds of readers are those who would actually buy your book in a bookstore. If you've written a sci-fi thriller and your wife only reads nineteenth-century British fiction, look for advice outside the home!

RULE 2: Don't send your manuscript to random agents. Much like finding readers, you'll want to find an agent who represents books like yours. To find this kind of agent, look in the acknowledgments section of books that are similar in voice, content, and spirit as yours. Authors often thank their agents in the acknowledgments. Once you've found at least a dozen agents, research them. Search the Web, read their online bios, look to see if they have Twitter feeds, and research whether they have been interviewed. See which ones feel like a potential match. Then, when you write your query letters, let them know why you think they're a good match and how your book fits in with the rest of their list.

RULE 3: Submit your query letter to multiple agents simultaneously. Otherwise, you could wait twenty-five years before you find an agent (see Rule 5). When querying an agent by email (which these days should be the vast majority of the time), paste in the first five pages of your manuscript so they can get a taste of your writing.

RULE 4: God is in the details. Make sure you've spelled the agent's name correctly. Proofread and spell-check your work. And always include all your contact info. If you're not detail-oriented, find someone who is to do a careful check of everything before you send it off.

RULE 5: Be patient. It's not unheard of for an agent to take a year—that's right, a year—to get back to a writer about his or her query or manuscript. So there's a lot of waiting involved when finding an agent. And, remember, just because you're not hearing anything doesn't mean bad news. On the other hand, don't be afraid to follow up, especially if an agent has requested your materials. A friendly call every other week is perfectly appropriate."

Rushed, utilitarian descriptions and atrociously stiff dialogue are both side effects of writing so much, so quickly.

In your rewrite, you have the wonderful opportunity to decorate your book with the kind of delicious linguistic flourishes that are inevitably lacking in a first draft. As you revise, be sure to vary your sentence lengths, and keep your descriptors vibrant. Watch for pat adjectives and similes like "ice-blue" eyes or minds that function "like steel traps." If your seas are roiling and your bosoms heaving, you should come up with fresher descriptions.

Your characters' conversations also likely suffered from the rush job. Look closely at every instance someone speaks: Is the language natural, realistic, and true to the character? I know that the loqua-ciousness of my characters corresponds directly with the amount I was behind on the week's word-count quota. Examine the content of dialogue, and ask yourself if each conversation is necessary to move the story forward or to help reveal the characters. If not, rewrite or cut them.

The other easily correctable, oft-seen problem with month-long novels concerns the props and cultural ephemera used in the background of the story. As you sketched your novel's scenery, you likely grabbed whatever materials were convenient at the time. Your protagonist may have been singing along to the songs playing on the radio as you wrote, and may have had long discussions about movies you'd recently seen or books you'd just read.

Oftentimes, these haphazard background elements will fit sur-prisingly well with your story. But during the editing process you should look skeptically at all these details and flourishes, particularly those that you copied and pasted from life around you. References to songs, movies, and other pieces of popular culture are all excellent ways to add layers of meaning to a novel, but when used sloppily, they tend to be more puzzling than powerful.

In the editing process, you'll also need to do those tiresome research and accuracy checks you wisely skipped when writing your rough draft. Do you have the rainy season sweeping through your Indonesian novel in the proper months? Do Finnish people really eat their weight in cupcakes every year? Where is Saskatoon, anyway? The internet likely has the answers to all your pressing fact-checking problems.

Next Steps: Publishing →

If you're planning on getting an agent for your book and going the tra-ditional publishing route, check out Arielle Eckstut's fantastic tips on page 186.

If you'd like to publish your own novel, you're in great company. Classic tomes such as *The Joy of Cooking* and James Joyce's *Ulysses* started out as self-published books. In the past few years, an increasing number of new and established authors have been using ebooks and print-on-demand technology to take their tales directly to readers.

The benefits of self-publishing are many. You get a *much* larger percentage of every sale, you have total creative control, and you're liberated from the publishing industry's glacially slow release schedules. Being the CEO of your own publishing endeavor nets you a ton of valuable business skills, and brings you into contact with a world of amazing people, from bloggers to illustrators to other self-published authors.

That said, forgoing an agent and publisher means you're giving up some nice perks. Self-published authors don't get advances. They have to cover the expenses a publisher normally absorbs, including copyediting and cover design. Most libraries and brick-and-mortar bookshops won't carry self-published books, and spreading the word about your book will involve a lot of hustling. Every hour you spend on administration will be one less hour you can spend writing.

To be fair, authors with big publishing houses behind them struggle with many of these same issues. To me, the biggest downside to self-publishing is that writers don't get help deciding when the book is done.

As Erin Morgenstern's story on page 184 illustrates, books get much better with each successive draft. At a certain point, you so have to stop futzing with the thing and just put it out there. As writers, though, we are notoriously bad judges of when we've reached that point. It's easy to confuse being fed up with a story with being finished with it. Helping you understand the difference between the two is where a good agent and editor are worth their weight in gold.

TIPS FROM THE TRENCHES:
NANOWRIMO WINNERS ON POST-NOVEL LIVING

"You're allowed to brag. It feels good to set your Facebook status to 'I wrote a book' and harvest the Likes and comments (you deserve it!)."
—**AMBER VALLANCE,** ONE-TIME NANOWRIMO WINNER FROM GHENT, BELGIUM

"Share your final word count. Everyone who was following your literary adventure will know what it stands for, and you can all celebrate together."
—**SARA HARRICHARAN,** SEVEN-TIME NANOWRIMO WINNER FROM PARROTTSVILLE, TENNESSEE

"I put a copy of my novel on a flash drive and hang it on a lanyard around my neck and walk around with a tired but happy smile on my face. It means nothing to anyone but myself."
—**SUZANNE ATKINS,** TEN-TIME NANOWRIMO WINNER FROM LONDON, UNITED KINGDOM

"If you still feel like you Should Be Doing Something each day, go ahead and do it. Use that, and conquer the world! Or at least your to-do list."
—**MARA JOHNSTONE,** TEN-TIME NANOWRIMO WINNER FROM SANTA ROSA, CALIFORNIA

"If you're like me, you'll have coursework to do, assignments to write, and housework. So don't collapse, even though you want to."
—**JACKI DRAYCOTT,** FIVE-TIME NANOWRIMO WINNER FROM BLACKPOOL, UNITED KINGDOM

"After the month is over, reduce your daily minimum word count to 500 until you reach the end of the story. Don't take a day off, just take some pressure off so that you can resume your old lifestyle."
—**DALE BARNARD,** TWO-TIME NANOWRIMO WINNER FROM AUSTIN, TEXAS

"Writing so quickly unleashes a torrent of ideas. Now that you have gotten used to corralling those brilliant, random thoughts, find another project that can channel your efforts in the same way."
—**ROLF NELSON,** FOUR-TIME NANOWRIMO WINNER FROM PROVIDENCE, RHODE ISLAND

"The truth is that there is no regular life after a month of noveling. You're a different type of person after writing a book in a month. You start to see the world from a different lens, one that looks at new challenges and says 'Yes, I CAN do this!'"
—**SUJIN HEADRICK,** ELEVEN-TIME NANOWRIMO WINNER FROM ATLANTA, GEORGIA

"Form a writing group. Meet once or twice a month, and bounce ideas off each other to keep your brain active and story ideas flowing."
—**MICHAEL SIROIS,** TEN-TIME NANOWRIMO WINNER FROM SPRING, TEXAS

"Take a good, long look at your bookshelf. You'll have a whole new appreciation for your favorite authors."
—**DENTON FROESE,** NINE-TIME NANOWRIMO WINNER FROM MEDICINE HAT, CANADA

"Spend a lot of time telling people how your novel turned out way better than you expected. Also, refuse to let anyone read it."
—**DAN STRACHOTA,** TWELVE-TIME NANOWRIMO WINNER FROM OAKLAND, CALIFORNIA

"Start calling yourself a writer."
—**REGINA KAMMER,** SEVEN-TIME NANOWRIMO WINNER FROM OAKLAND, CALIFORNIA

"After sleeping for as long as humanly possible without technically entering a coma, I take stock of the activities that I dropped during the intense focus of NaNoWriMo and usually decide not to pick them back up again, other than those things required for survival and staying married."
—**KAREN WILLSHER,** EIGHT-TIME NANOWRIMO WINNER FROM EDMONTON, CANADA

"As for the transition back to normal life, sometimes it doesn't happen. Sometimes you get the strength to retire early or change careers so that you can continue to write. I just sold a short and have an agent for one of my NaNo-novels. I ain't going back."
—**KATHY KITTS,** TEN-TIME NANOWRIMO WINNER FROM PLACITAS, NEW MEXICO

A Final Thought →

Whenever I talk about how much work editing requires, I frequently hear this lament from NaNoWriMo participants: "With the book market so tight, no agent is going to take a chance on me. And if I self-publish, I'll just be another voice in a sea of authors struggling to find an audience. With the odds of success so low, why bother editing?"

When faced with this question, I think of my friend Brent. Brent is an environmental engineer, and his weekdays are filled with incredibly complex mathematical equations.

On weekends, Brent plays softball.

Brent is not the greatest softball player. Brent played volleyball in college on his school's team, and he's a slamming, spiking terror at the net. He's also a force to be reckoned with on the basketball court.

On the softball diamond, though, Brent has a lot to learn. Which is partly why he does it. To challenge himself. To grow. The pitchers of beer after the game don't hurt, either.

Anyway, whenever people express their reluctance to invest time in something that won't have proven results, I ask them what they do for fun on weekends.

Invariably, the time they spend running around on basketball courts, rearranging Scrabble tiles, or slaying video-game monsters is not done in an effort to make millions of dollars from corporate sponsorships. Or because they think it will make them famous.

No. They do it because the challenge of the game simply feels good. They do it because they like to compete; because they like spending time with friends; because it feels really, really nice to just lose themselves in the visceral pleasure of an activity.

Novel writing is just a recreational sport where you don't have to get up out of your chair. And that's exactly how I encourage writers to approach revisions. As you edit, do it in the spirit of a playground softball game. No stakes, no pressure. No one in the stands watching or judging. Just you versus a dozen easily distracted, unathletic third-graders who will believe anything you say about outs and ups because they think you're the gym teacher.

Okay, forget that part about the third-graders. But you know what I'm saying. Don't waste your time thinking about the agents, the publishers, or the market. It's just you, and it's just for fun. And, should things go well, you'll have a convenient paper record of your heroic deeds to share for decades to come.

But even if this book doesn't pan out, there's always the next one. And the one after that. So go for it. Take risks and swing for the fences. The game begins anew every day, and it only gets better from here.

Acknowledgments

Thanks, first and foremost, to Wendy Ginsburg, for all the love and support. You make my life a better place, and I look forward to writing a 50,000-word novel celebrating your beauty and wisdom this November. On a scale of 1 to 5, you are a 6.

A huge thank-you to National Novel Writing Month participants and Municipal Liaisons worldwide, and to NaNoWriMo's staff and board in Berkeley. Special thanks to OLL'ers Grant Faulkner, Tavia Stewart-Streit, Sarah Mackey, Chris Angotti, Tim Kim, Dan Duvall, Jezra Lichter, Heather Dudley, Emily Bristow, Lindsey Grant, Jennifer Arzt, Cybele May, Cylithria Dubois, Christopher White, Eric Doherty, Elizabeth Gregg, Tony Shen, Kara Platoni, Jason Snell, Russ Uman, and Ellen Martin.

I'm incredibly grateful to pep-talkers Gayle Brandeis, Rachael Herron, Marissa Meyer, Lani Diane Rich, Julia Crouch, Elizabeth Haynes, Sara Gruen, and Erin Morgenstern. Thanks as well to Genn Albin, who kindly agreed to contribute a pep talk but was felled by illness at the last minute.

I'd like to give a shout-out to my Chronicle Books editor Wynn Rankin (fearless keeper of the One Manuscript to Rule Them All), and the great Sarah Malarkey. Designer Tatiana Pavlova and copyeditor extraordinaire Kathie Gordon were invaluable in making the book better. And big tip of the hat to all the Chronicle Books editors I've worked with over the years: Emilie Sandoz, Jennifer Kong, Leslie Jonath, and Jeff Campbell.

Mighty thanks to Lindsay Edgecombe and everyone at Levine Greenberg, including inimitable agent-at-large Arielle Eckstut.

Hugs to the folks featured in the 2004 edition who are making a return appearance ten years later: Dan Strachota (who gave great advice throughout this updating process), Tim Lohnes, Trena Taylor, Amy Probst, Karla Akins, Erin Allday, Rise Sheridan-Peters, Jennifer McCreedy, Irfon-Kim Ahmad, Andrew Johnson, Carolyn Lawrence, Michele Marques, Carol McBay, and Peter Abel.

A gigantic thanks to all the NaNoWriMo winners who sent in advice to be included in the new edition of the book. I sadly didn't have room to include everyone's genius tips, but your names shall stand here as a testament to your brilliance: Aeryn Brown, Agatha Tan, Alex McGilvery, Alexa Schmidt, Ali Hawke, Alicia Wallace, Aliyah Weinstein, Allison Barclay, Amanda Qu, Amber Vallance, Amy Rohozen, Angela Lindfors, Anita King, Anna Rudolf, Ashley Martin, Barbara Neill, Ben Byriel, Beth Carter, C. A. Bridges, Caitlin Perry, Candice Robinson, Carmen Fowle, Carmen Young, Chelsea Ekholm, Chris Olinger, Christina Weigand, Courtney Richards, Cyrene Krey, Dale Barnard, Danni Lawrence, Darlene Reilley, Dawn Laker, Denton Froese, E. Kristin Anderson, Elia Winters, Emily Bristow, Emily Hogarth, Eva Da'mole, Gabrielle Stepp, Gale Hathcock Albright, Heather Caprio, Heather Millard, Hilary Oudyk, Imaan Asri, Jacki Draycott, Jamie Ihrer, Jamie Phillips, Jane Ormond, Jane Rawson, Jean Anderson, Jennie Vongvith, Jessica Boulay, Jessica Gaines, Joanna Askutja, Jonathan Ferguson, Kain Foran, Karen Willsher, Katharine Stubbs, Kathryn Marshall, Kathy Kitts, Kayla Marnach, Kelly Greene, Kristin Prinz, Lauren Coffin, Lauren Hopkins Karcz, Lesley Morgan, Letitia Jones, Lieke Braadbaart, Lindsay Gilmour, Louise Cole, Lucy Ralston, Madeline Turnipseed, Malerie Anderson, Mandi M. Lynch, Mara Johnstone, Mari Myllykangas, Marrije Schaake, May Chong, Melanie Macek, Melinda Primrose, Michael Bergeron, Michael Sirois, Michelle Breckon, Molly Mungons, Morgan Hyde, Nicole Dumasy, Nicole Palmby, Nicole Tuberty, Nyla Nox, Olivia Coackley, Pam Gray, Patience Virtue, Patricia Pinto, Paula White, Paz Alonso, Peg Rousar-Thompson, Phyllis Penninga, Poh Wee Chern, Rachel Lightfoot, Regina Kammer, Richenda Gould, Rolf Nelson, Rose Dawson, Rose Sorooshian, Royce Roeswood, Sabrina Panetta, Saker Pup, Sara Harricharan, Sarah Haines, Sarah Parks, Skye Woestehoff, Sonia Rao, Sophia Volpi, Sophie Boyce, Stefan Ecks, Stephanie B., Stephanie Kelly, Stéphanie Noël, Steven Hoffman, Sujin Headrick, Suzanne Atkins, Syahira Sharif, Sydney

NO PLOT? NO PROBLEM!

Hoffa, Tim Yao, Tom Challis, Tommie Colombaroni, Trini Quiroz, and Trudy Goold.

Finally, I would like to gratefully acknowledge my trusty Dell Latitude laptop, Peet's Coffee, llamas, eucalyptus trees, Casa Sanchez medium salsa, sliced deli ham, the chicken tikka masala at House of Curries in Berkeley, and the late-night taquerias of the Greater Bay Area. Your light is a beacon to us all.

NOTES

NOTES

NOTES